Best Wishes
Bob Englebrecht

# for the
# LOVE
## of
# MARRIAGE

# for the
# LOVE
## of
# MARRIAGE

## John M. Drescher

Intercourse, PA 17534
800/762-7171
www.goodbks.com

Cover design and illustration by Cheryl Benner
Design by Dawn J. Ranck

Good Books, Intercourse, PA 17534
International Standard Book Number: 1-56148-168-8
Library of Congress Catalog Card Number: 96-1104

**Library of Congress Cataloging-in-Publication Data**

Drescher, John M.
    For the love of marriage / John M. Drescher.
       p. cm.
    ISBN 1-56148-168-8
    1. Marriage. I. Title.
HQ734.D844   1996
30681--dc20                                        96-1104
                                                   CIP

To our five children
and their spouses
and their children,
who are much in my thoughts
as I write what is important to me now.

# Table of Contents

# About This Book

Getting married is not difficult. Millions marry every year. And each couple expects to live happily ever after as the fairy tales promise.

But getting married doesn't guarantee anything. As we all know, it takes much more than a marriage certificate or a beautiful church ceremony to make a marriage meaningful and happy. A wedding certificate is more like a learner's permit. A happy marriage is for those who are committed to traveling together—through the barren valleys as well as over the blissful heights.

Marriage is a relationship—a relationship *in process*. And a loving, living, growing marriage is a lifelong vocation. A mature, satisfying marriage takes time, hard work, and the constant, caring cooperation of two persons committed to sharing and to caring, to loving and to listening, to giving and to forgiving, to encouraging until death parts. A successful marriage is constantly monitored, adjusted, and nourished.

Difficulties or differences will definitely show up soon after the wedding vows are said. And a couple who is ready to give up because of the struggles will never experience a happy marriage. Happy marriages are reserved for those who know the security of sticking together through drudgery and delight, for better or for worse, during the expected and the unexpected.

No precise formula exists which promises perfect married bliss. No perfect marriage partner ever lived. There are happy and satisfying marriages, but they do not just happen. Happy marriages are the result of concerted effort and clear commitment. They grow out of a commitment to love, to care for another as much as one cares for oneself, to look for and expect the best, and to live in the light of the Creator's vision for marriage.

Many of the ideas I discuss here grow from hundreds of husband-and-wife retreats and seminars I've led through the years. I've tried out many of these thoughts with thousands of husbands and wives, and also with many couples in premarital counseling.

Whenever we have the chance to discuss these ideas, they seem to spark great interest. Time and again I have been asked, "Why don't you put all of this in a book to help others?" Or, "Make it available for those who can't attend or afford a retreat."

Sometimes parents say, "Don't you think persons should be told these things before marriage?" Yes, I do think young people should be told, and I do find myself offering much of this whenever I have opportunity.

I am convinced that although it may be hard for a couple to believe these ideas are true before they are married, they will be better prepared when they face the reality of wedded life if they have thought about these matters.

At the close of each section of the book are questions for couples or groups to talk about. What I find is that in such discussions, persons often rediscover hope. Many couples think that no other marriage has the same problems as theirs does. So they feel hopeless.

In groups we soon see that our problems are not unique, and we begin to see possibilities for resolving them. One evening after I finished talking about differences and the difficulties they create, I asked for questions and observations from anyone in the group. One husband, perhaps forty years old, asked with a deep sigh of relief, "Do you mean that others went through the same thing we did?"

The group laughed together with him. We have all, I believe, gone through the same or similar problems to one degree or another.

Then from the group came one story after another. By the end of the evening, couples felt renewed hope because for the first time they saw that their problems weren't unique. If others could work out similar problems and experience a happy and radiant relationship, they could, too. May such an experience be yours as you read and discuss these pages.

After being married more than forty years, I simply want to share some of the hard, as well as the wonderful, lessons Betty and I have learned and are still learning. I am committed to helping couples avoid the pitfalls and pains of a poor marriage and to experience the deep joys and satisfactions of a happy and meaningful marriage.

Betty and I tell each other continually that our love today is greater and stronger and deeper than we could ever have imagined in our early years together. Our marriage hasn't always been easy, but we believe our differences and difficulties helped to forge our deeper love as we determined to stick together through it all. I want to address these enduring elements in the hope that someone, somewhere, will be blessed with a fulfilling marriage.

—John M. Drescher

# I.

# The Drama of Marriage

# 1.
# The Drama Begins

*"How beautiful you are my love, how very beautiful! . . . You are altogether beautiful, my love; there is no flaw in you."*

—Song of Solomon 4:1, 7

Years ago in England, ten-year-old William Montage Dyke was blinded by an accident. William went through university and, though blind, graduated with honors. During his university days he dated a beautiful girl and they decided to get married. William, of course, never saw his bride.

Some months before the wedding, a skilled eye surgeon put William through a series of tests and treatments. On the day of his wedding, his father took him to the church with his eyes still covered with bandages. William's bride Jennifer entered the church on the arm of her white-haired father. As she moved to the altar, while the soft strains of Lohengrin's wedding march floated through the church, she saw a surprising sight.

The eye surgeon stood beside William, cutting away the last bandage. Recovering from the shock, William steadied himself and, with obvious joy, stepped forward to meet his bride.

It is difficult to imagine that dramatic moment as the bridegroom saw his bride for the first time at the marriage altar! Yet something similar happens in every wedding. Most brides and grooms have seen each other many times before meeting at the altar. Yet part of the drama of every wedding is that, regardless of how well a couple may think they know each other, regardless of how beautiful or handsome each may be, there is still much they are blind to.

Only as each of us enters the intimacy of marriage are our eyes opened. We see each other in a new and different way. Many years ago Alexander Pope said: "They dream in courtship but in wedlock wake." It takes a lifetime to see each other truly, to understand each other, and to love each other as God intends and as we deeply desire.

One of the great excitements of being married is realizing that it will take many years of loving and living to learn to know each other. A good marriage will have unimagined joy, unexpected depths of love, and unanticipated experiences and trials—all of which have the capacity to bind and build a couple into a growing oneness.

In Solomon's love song in the Old Testament, a groom extols the beauty of his bride. In his love she looks perfect. She is without a flaw. And that is part of the wonder of pure love. But an even greater miracle of love happens when we see our partner's imperfections, yet we continue to grow more deeply in love than we ever imagined on the day of our wedding. This is the drama of marriage.

### For further thought:

> I one time asked a Marriage Retreat group, "How much do you think you knew each other when you got married?" Finally, a man married approximately forty years spoke up. "I think I knew my wife about seven percent."

> Discuss how much you think you knew your spouse at the time of your marriage. What has learning to know each other since then meant?

# 2.

# *For Bitter or For Better*

A group of film producers listed the ten most dramatic sounds in the movies: (1) a baby's first cry, (2) the blast of a siren, (3) the thunder of breakers on rocks, (4) the roar of a forest fire, (5) a foghorn, (6) the slow drip of water, (7) galloping horses, (8) a distant train whistle, (9) the howl of a dog, and (10) the "Wedding March."

The group claimed that of these ten, one sound causes more emotional responses and upheaval than any other. It brings on a range of powerful feelings—sadness, envy, regret, sorrow, tears, and supreme joy. It is—you guessed it!—the "Wedding March."

When two people stand before the altar to "become one" in marriage, they enter one of the most emotional associations within human experience. Two completely different personalities come together for life. They consummate the original union that God intended as "the two becoming one flesh."

Perhaps the "Wedding March" draws such powerful emotions from us because we know that marriage, more than any other relationship in life, can make us either bitter or better. Some partners in the intimacy of marriage draw the worst disposition, traits, and character from each other. Marriage diminishes these persons. After years together, some husbands and wives seem to know less of each other than when they began.

Yet other couples call the best from each other through the closeness of their marriage companionship. We know that they are better persons now than they could ever have been alone.

Whether we become bitter or better persons has nothing to do with the *amount* of difficulties, differences, or adjustments in our marriage. All marriages have plenty of these. If handled well, difficulties and differences can draw a couple together and add dimension to life. Or they can disrupt and drive partners apart if they deal with their struggles poorly.

In a happy marriage, each spouse tries to deal with difficulties in a sympathetic, caring, and open way. Partners search together for solutions, rather than responding to trouble with vindication, blame, or escape.

We will have satisfying marriages when we move from self-centeredness to interdependent love, when we truly realize our need for each other. Such maturing is a gradual process, not an attitude that arrives in a short time. It is a movement away from being preoccupied with one's self and the satisfying of one's own desires to a concern for the other. We are born male and female. But we grow to be mature men and women, husbands and wives.

As we mature together, each of us individually grows to better understand our own selves. Why am I the way I am? Why do I respond the way I do? Who am I? This personal growth can enrich and enhance our marriages.

We also need a realistic understanding of love. Love is not something which hits us out of the blue and then stays with us forever. While we might be *attracted* at first sight, we will never *love* at first sight. Love is more like a plant. If it is fed and nurtured and continually cultivated, it grows into something beautiful. Without that, it dries up and dies, no matter how good the soil, how special the seed, or how well planted it was at the start.

If your spouse is beautiful or handsome at twenty-five, you can't take any credit. But if your spouse is beautiful or handsome at fifty-five, you might be partly responsible!

So how are we to become better, not bitter, persons in our marriages?

**For further thought:**
> What do you think is necessary if we are to become better persons rather than bitter persons in marriage?

# 3.
# *Similarities Are Significant*

We all know marriages that we predicted would fail. Why did we say or feel that way? Did we simply conclude that the two people were too different, too unlike each other, to succeed in marriage?

Why do persons marry the persons they do? Do people marry for love? Is there hope for a marriage if the partners seem incompatible?

No marriage will succeed without the two persons working willingly and continually at it. Yet it is true that the more alike two spouses are in certain areas, the better chance they have for a good start, at least. Look first at sociological similarities.

Similar *religious backgrounds* are important. Many persons head for matrimonial difficulty because they don't face their religious differences or deal with them honestly.

The divorce rate is up to five times higher for mixed marriages than for those in which both spouses come from the same or similar religious groups. After they marry, couples from different religious backgrounds often stop attending church and observing their individual religious practices. Some mixed marriages succeed, but only if couples make continuing and concerted efforts, if they work to deal with their differences constructively, and if they are willing to compromise fairly.

As children come along, religious differences usually seem to grow bigger. Too many persons assume that they will work at these matters after the wedding, only to find that the chasm which separates them seems too large, or the effort to build the necessary bridge too frustrating and irritating.

If either partner cares seriously about religion or faith, that couple needs to face squarely their religious differences before they marry. Our feelings and interest in faith and religion usually become more serious as we mature.

Too great a *difference in economic outlook* also presents problems. While a couple may be persuaded before marrying that "Love solves all," they find after marriage that it is not that simple. About half of those who marry have fairly close agreement and a common understanding on economic matters—how to get, spend, save, give, and use their money. The other fifty percent are at odds and discover that the wider their difference, the more difficult their adjustment. A large percentage of couples seeking divorce are heavily in debt.

Laura was from an upper middle class family. While in college, Laura met Tom, who was struggling financially as a student. Laura and Tom were attracted to each other and got married during their junior year of college. Laura's parents had always paid her bills, so she had little sense of what things cost and almost no experience in pinching pennies. Laura and Tom had talked some about what marriage would mean financially. And they decided to struggle on their own, rather than become dependent upon their parents.

After several months, the financial squeeze became so intense that they needed to decide whether one should drop out for a semester or a year and work. The tension only grew when Laura, who didn't need to worry about money before marriage, bought things Tom thought weren't essential. Then Laura's parents visited, saw their scarce furnishings, and learned about Laura and Tom's difficult financial situation. Within less than six months, this couple's relationship was under great stress from a variety of quarters.

A *similar cultural background* enhances the promise of a couple's satisfactory adjustment in marriage. Several generations ago most people married someone from their neighborhood. Today that rarely happens. We are a highly mobile society, and we cross community, state, and even country borders as we go to school, change jobs, or simply travel. As a result, many of us choose a marriage partner from a background different from our own.

Before marrying a person of a different cultural background or race, it is quite helpful to live for a time in the other's cultural setting. It is one way to begin to understand many of the unspoken assumptions and intricacies which soon show up after marriage.

### For further thought:

> *How are you and your spouse similar or dissimilar in the areas discussed in this chapter?*

# 4.
# *Additional Similarities*

Some differences between spouses are obvious. Other differences can only be discovered through a day-to-day relationship in a variety of settings.

Too great a spread in *educational backgrounds and experiences* can cause difficulty. A chaplain in a large university observed that one of the major reasons couples split up following graduate school is their different amounts of education. In many cases the wife slaves away, earning the family income while her husband gets his degree. They both work long and late and spend little time together. They look forward to the years following school when they can settle down and enjoy each other. But when the graduate work is completed, they suddenly find they have little to talk about and little in common. The husband has developed his intellectual world, while his wife has not. They are miles apart in what they care about and understand.

Other important sociological similarities include those of *age and interests* in life. Increasingly, as I counsel single young people, as well as couples whose marriages are in trouble, I have come to believe that common interests are exceedingly important for a happy marriage. A couple who has little that they like to do together is greatly handicapped. They have relatively little sense of togetherness; they may not really enjoy each other's company. They don't naturally find pleasure from participating in each other's joys.

If a married couple discovers that they have few common

interests, they should immediately look for areas which they find satisfying together. When this happens, both can experience a sense of blessing and achievement.

I remember one couple who had almost no common interests. During their years of child-rearing and work, they lived very separate lives. It was during retirement, when many couples find it difficult to be together for twenty-four hours a day, that this pair found several things they enjoyed doing together. Those experiences opened an entirely new existence for them.

What seemed destined to be a lonely survival of each other and retirement, suddenly became a life of excitement and enjoyment which they had never experienced before. They discovered common ground in a few simple pleasures, and that made the difference between their enduring—or enjoying—each other. It enriched all of their life together.

Here is one of the great opportunities of marriage. Some couples grow in oneness as they find common interests in particular activities. Some discover a spiritual oneness through learning to give themselves to God and in offering service to others.

Marrying a spouse who is much younger or older, or marrying a person with significantly different interests in life, does not make a happy marriage impossible, but it does make it more difficult. The more sociological similarities between a couple, the better their beginning, the more likely their chances of a satisfying future. Differences can drive very sincere lovers apart, and those differences become increasingly dramatic after the wedding day.

### For further thought:

> *How are the similarities mentioned in this chapter present or not present in your marriage? What are examples of other similarities which are important in making a satisfying marriage?*

# 5.

# *But Opposites Attract*

Donna and Bob had a good start when it came to sociological similarities. Yet they had a lot of trouble because they were so different in temperament. As Bob explained it: "We thought we were very much alike before marriage. We were made for each other. But after marriage we found we were very, very different. How could two people so opposite be attracted to each other?"

Donna and Bob had been in numerous discussions about their religious backgrounds, their economic outlooks, their cultural heritages. But they were helped most by a discussion about their psychological makeups. They began to see how these make or break a marriage. Their psychological differences were at the root of their difficulties. Donna said, "Many times we felt we were not made for each other. It was a great relief to realize that in matters of temperament human beings often choose persons to marry who are quite different from themselves. In fact, God made us this way so that we might grow together and become bigger persons than we could ever be alone."

These psychological differences are just as important to consider as sociological ones. I have found through my contacts with hundreds of couples that an understanding of these factors can be of immense value and help in working through all kinds of painful problems in marriage.

Whenever I hear the word "incompatibility," I have a strange negativism rise within me, especially when it is used to explain two persons not getting along. In marriage it is sometimes used as an excuse for separation. People suddenly imagine or are told that they are "incompatible."

Who is "compatible," if it means that two people see everything alike, always agree, are at the same emotional level, have similar temperaments, or will grow in love without struggle?

Paul Tournier's statement in *To Understand Each Other* rings true: "So-called emotional incompatibility is a myth invented by jurists short of arguments in order to plead for divorce. It is likewise a common excuse people use in order to hide their own feelings. I simply do not believe it exists. There are no emotional incompatibilities. There are misunderstandings and mistakes, however, which can be corrected when there is a willingness to do so."

Urban Steinmetz, a marriage and family counselor in Escanaba, Michigan, says, "I have never yet met a compatible couple." Cecil G. Osborne in *Understanding Your Mate* says that the basic assumption we should have is "incompatibility." What do Tournier, Steinmetz, and Osborne mean?

Should persons marry compatible partners? The answer is "Yes," if we are speaking only of sociological factors such as cultural background, age, religious beliefs, economic outlook, and educational level. Counselors generally agree that when persons marry and are dissimilar in these areas, their differences will become more dramatic after marriage and can create real difficulties in adjustment and understanding.

If, however, we are referring to compatibility or similarity in psychological traits, the answer to the question, "Should persons marry compatible partners?" is "No!" Almost without exception, people marry their opposites in areas of temperament and psychological makeup.

Opposites do attract, and to marry someone who is psychologically the same or very similar would, at best, stifle chances for growth and lead to boredom in marriage.

Studies by Dr. Joseph Wheelwright of San Francisco show that most people in his test samples marry their complete opposites when it comes to temperament. Wheelwright writes, "People marry people they'd never dream of having as friends."

Though we may give little or no thought to it in courtship or even after marriage, we are naturally drawn to persons who are strong where we are weak. God made us this way. Unconsciously, we seek fulfillment in someone who personifies what we do not possess and, therefore, deeply desire. This is what we mean when we speak of certain traits being complementary. This is what is meant when we say "opposites attract."

In fact, this desire for a person who has what we do not have is so strong, that we might correctly say persons marry not so much for love, as for fulfillment, for completeness, and for self-improvement.

### For further thought:

*Do you agree that incompatibility in marriage is a myth, and that we are drawn to marry our opposites temperamentally, at least in a number of major areas?*

# 6.
# *Give Me More Examples*

In practical terms, what does this mean? It means that an active person usually chooses to marry someone who is more passive. But differences in physical energy can cause trouble. A person who is rarin' to go may resent needing to slow down for the other. The more passive person may chafe about being dragged around and pushed beyond strength or desire.

An extrovert marries an introvert. An impulsive person marries a calm, collected companion. A talkative person marries one who is quiet (both can't talk simultaneously!). A perfectionist marries one who is almost careless.

Recently at a retreat a wife spoke about her husband as being extremely analytical, while she, by contrast, couldn't care less about analyzing everything someone says or does. A procrastinator usually marries a person who must always have things done on time. Someone who is punctual and must be on time everywhere marries a partner who fits this description by a frustrated husband: "I just have to believe in a second resurrection. My wife would never make the first one."

Then there is the day person who would choose to go to bed by 8:00 and is ready to get up with the sun. Such an individual marries a night person, one who gets started about mid-afternoon and is going strong at midnight, but finds it difficult to get out of bed before 10:00 or 11:00 a.m. A tightfisted miser marries a spendthrift.

On and on the list goes. Neatniks marry slobs; elk-hunting husbands marry women who write poetry; affectionate women marry aloof men and vice versa; gregarious and impulsive persons marry reticent and inhibited partners. The rationalizer marries the sentimentalist and the practical person marries the dreamer.

So it is obvious that we are drawn, in a dramatic way, to marry those who are opposite from us temperamentally. We are fascinated by the person who can do what we cannot. We are attracted to the person who displays personal qualities we desire but do not have. We are drawn to the person who demonstrates strength where we are weak. And this happens even though we never take a minute to consider it.

We are clearly in search of completeness. God made us so that marriage partners can complement each other. One makes up for what the other lacks; the two lend strength to each other. Therefore, marriage has greater possibilities for growth than any other relationship in life if we accept these differences between us and if we are able to respond properly. When marriage partners continue to value and cultivate the strength each brings, they have numerous possibilities for personal and marital development and happiness.

Our psychological differences give us a sense of belonging to each other. As we grow to appreciate these differences, we increasingly grow together. We inwardly detect, even though we may have never consciously considered it, that we need the other to be complete. It is this sense, when developed properly, which makes us feel "He belongs to me" or "She belongs to me."

An older couple approached me after a meeting. The husband put his arm around his wife and said to me with a deep love, "She belongs to me." She put her arm around him and said with the same loving expression, "Yes, and he also belongs to me."

What gave that sense of belonging? Certainly not that they were alike. They were very different persons temperamentally. But, over the years, they had learned to accept and adjust and appreciate the qualities of each other, and it gave them the sense of belonging which each of us needs.

**For further thought:**

> *What differences in your temperaments are apparent to you now?*

# 7.
# *Differences Can Divide—*
# *Or Draw Together*

There never was a marriage that could not have been a failure. Elements of disharmony are present in every marriage. On the other hand, there are few, if any, marriages which could not be a success, if two people are determined to make it so.

What happens in many marriages, soon after the promises are exchanged, is that differences begin to divide rather than draw together. What attracted us now distracts us; what drew us together now tends to drive us apart. Because we don't understand our differences or their value, coldness and loneliness enter and begin to destroy the relationship. Instead of seeing that differences can add dimension, and that together we can be stronger than we are alone, we begin to say, "You're not like I am," or "You're just like your mother," or "We aren't compatible."

The old line seems right—"What caught attention before marriage creates tension after marriage." This is true if we do not allow our partner to continue to be the person we chose. If we do not see that differences can add dimension rather than drive us apart. If we fail to see that we need our partner, with all his or her qualities, to make us strong and complete. If we do not learn to bring out the strengths in each other while overcoming our own weaknesses.

A friend of mine, Dr. Abraham Schmitt, psychologist and

family counselor, told me that when couples come to him because they believe they are incompatible, he asks them what first attracted them to each other. "Invariably," he said, "each mentions the very things which are now driving them apart." The husband says, "I guess I liked her free, outgoing spirit. She wasn't always busy with details; she could enjoy herself in a group. I was always rather shy." But now his complaint is that she never gets things done. She is always distracted, visiting neighbors, helping some group, forgetting her family. She doesn't even clean her own house.

What does she say about her husband? She says she loved his concern for detail. He was calm. She liked particularly how he paid attention to his clothes and that he kept his car clean. "He was careful and courteous before marriage." Now she finds him difficult to live with. "He is always bothered by the appearance of the house, that the beds aren't made and the dishes aren't done immediately. He's more concerned about *things* than persons."

Each needed the other to complement his or her own weaknesses. But instead of sharing the strengths each brought, they began to do battle over the very things for which they chose each other. A man likes a prim, carefully manicured, and attractively dressed woman. After marriage he complains that it takes her half a day to get dressed for a dinner appointment.

Picture a self-contained, reflective man, given to choosing his words carefully, who marries a woman of ready wit and tongue, quick on the trigger and vibrant to her fingertips. When someone asks him a question, he doesn't get a chance to answer. While he pauses to think, his wife launches a graphic response to the question.

What does this do in time, if it is continually repeated? The husband begins to doubt himself. Perhaps he becomes reluctant to enter a conversation. Inside he resents his wife speaking for him, while she continues, oblivious to it all.

Picture a reserved and quiet woman, slow to enter into activities and conversations. She is quite capable, but always needs urging before she gains the confidence to accept responsibility. She is married to a very competent, aggressive man who, after marriage, begins to see her hesitancy as a liability. He doesn't understand that she needs support and encouragement more than criticism, if she is to develop initiative. By his response he makes her more and more withdrawn.

### For further thought:

*What are those areas which you find yourself evading or not discussing with your spouse?*

# 8.
# *Differences Become Dramatic*

A couple comes for counsel. They are on the verge of breaking up. He says that before they were married, he liked her personality. She was caring, loving, and willing to listen. Yet she knew where she stood and had strong convictions. He liked her self-confidence. Now he finds her to be just like her mother, concerned about everything, defensive, sticking to her points of view without considering his.

She liked his easygoing ways while they were dating. She got uptight easily; he was calm and collected. "Plus, " she says, "I liked his self-control in contrast to my father who was quick to get angry." Now she complains that her husband doesn't notice things that need to be done around the house. The children can misbehave; he never notices. He is so easygoing that she must assume all responsibility around home.

Extroverts who love and live for fellowship and activity marry introverts who seek tranquility and serious thought. Carl Jung has shown that reason and sentiment are at opposite poles, as are intuition and realism. Instinctively, a rational man marries a sentimental woman. These complementary traits will, at first, stimulate each party. But later on the husband will try to make his wife pay attention to objective arguments. He will become irritated at his failure to get her to listen to reason. He will work to convince her that her sentimental outbursts are irrational. She will scold him because his rational approach robs life of the warmth she needs.

Personalities differ, but, in addition to that, men and women tend to approach life with different impulses and interests. Many men enjoy communicating ideas and programs and plans. Most women like to talk about feelings and emotions. Some researchers suggest that men and women actually speak two different languages.

A wife may be able to help her husband be more empathetic and to express his emotions more openly. While a wife may think of expressing love in words, her husband may be more inclined to express his love by doing things. Women tend to notice details; they are likely to recount the day's particulars—who said what and how people looked. Men may highlight events in more general, overall terms, growing somewhat impatient with details. If each spouse takes time to listen to the other, each will learn much and grow in a broader understanding of life. Taking time to understand each other builds communication, appreciation—and the relationship.

Unless we are aware of the role our psychological differences play in marriage, we will be driven apart by the very things which we need from each other to be complete and fulfilled.

Because we differ in ideas and behavior patterns, we try to remake our mates. I'd like my spouse to be more like me. Instead of accepting, loving, and helping each other to become better persons, we set out to change each other. When we sense that someone is trying to remake us, we all respond the same way. We dig in our heels. We react negatively and resist each other. We close up and don't talk.

Only as we are accepted and loved, do we find it possible to change. At times we may change some of our spouse's behavior by constantly nagging or complaining. But seldom, if ever, does such *behavioral* change bring about *inner* change or a better relationship. It is a coerced change, and it creates inner, growing bitterness, hostility, and withdrawal.

A marriage counselor, Ira J. Tanner, writes: "Any attempt to move one's mate in an effort to match them to our fantasies is arrogance on our part and an insult to them. It divides, breeds anger, and causes even greater loneliness."

If we do not want our marriage to be a failure, we must give up the goal of changing each other. It never works. When we set out to change each other rather than accept each other, we bring out the worst rather than the best. In addition, we may each develop feelings of guilt, leading to more and more estrangement and lack of communication.

When coldness grows between us and communication thins, we begin to dream secretly about the kind of partner we wish we had. We find ourselves ignoring the partner we do have. We develop a fantasy world rather than coming to grips with life. We fall in love with an image (maybe inspired by a soap opera or a colleague at work), instead of giving love to our partner. This leads many to divorce and marry another, who, because of the way we are made, will probably be much like the first person we married. And we will continue to run away from problems rather than face ourselves.

### For further thought:

*Do you agree that one of the greatest temptations in marriage is the desire to change the other? Can you give illustrations?*

# 9.
# *Disillusionment Descends*

"Eighteen months after our all-glorious wedding we hit a dip which I never imagined possible. I never knew such hurt. At times I thought I loved Jim, and at times I was sure I never could love him again. In my worst moments I thought I never loved him in the first place."

These words from a young wife sound painful and shocking. The truth is that every marriage, to some degree or another, experiences what this woman describes. Some speak of it as a period of despair. Others discuss it as a time of disillusionment. This wife describes it as "a dip," a good, descriptive word.

Regardless of what you call it, it happens in every vital marriage. In fact, I recently saw a book which begins by telling the readers not to read further unless they feel their getting married was a big mistake.

Before their weddings, many couples picture being married as one continuous climb into ecstasy, joy, and love. Songs, sermons, and stories leave the impression that marriage is truly living happily ever after.

The wedding vows are much more true and realistic: "Do you take this person for better and for worse?" That "worse" is likely to be very real and unromantic. Why? Because each of us has a worse side. Each of us has faults. Someone remarked, "What looked wonderful in the moonlight looks different in the sunlight." So the problem is not so much that we have faults. The problem is what we do about them.

If our spouses don't meet the images we absorb from commercials, advertisements, TV shows, and movies, we may be dissatisfied with our partners without even realizing why.

Marriage is real. And the reality of marriage is that each of us has faults. The sooner we admit them and accept the fact, the more content we will be. And the sooner we work at our own faults rather than trying to correct our spouse's, the more change we will see for the better.

H.G. Wells wrote, "A day arrives in every marriage when the lovers must face each other, disillusioned, stripped of the last shred of excitement—undisguisedly themselves."

Because of the many false notions we have about being married, we may enter marriage with many wrong suppositions. When the young wife's experience of marriage after eighteen months was so contrary to her expectations, her first thought was to file for divorce. "All is lost," she thought. "The marriage was a mistake; the best thing to do is get out."

The truth is that every marriage, to one degree or another, hits a dip. It may be in three months or in three years. Most dips occur during the first five years. Since every marriage hits a dip, it is better to recognize and deal with it than to deny it and run away. Those marriage partners who recognize the dip and work through it will have a stronger marriage in the end. Such a marriage can survive the little ups and downs which all marriages have.

**For further thought:**

*Do you agree that every marriage, to one degree or another, hits the "after-marriage dip"? What has your experience been?*

# 10.
## Unrealistic Expectations

The intimacy of marriage brings out those weaknesses and undesirable traits of ours which were not as apparent before. Soon we discover that each of us has a less desirable side. We often make unreasonable demands on each other—demands that would drive all our friends away if we asked the same of them.

Two dangers face us. One is to expect too much, even perfection! We carry the myths we had before marriage—the myths of complete compatibility, of having the perfect marriage partner, of being in a model marriage. The sooner we get rid of these fantasies, the better. They are myths, nothing else.

A second danger is that we may expect too little. We may not see the good in each other. Consequently, we don't expect and encourage each other to improve. Critical words and disapproving glances become a pattern. Or we focus on a negative trait and forget the many good ones.

We chose each other because we felt understood by the other. That feeling of being understood comes through talking, listening, and sharing. After marriage, all too often, partners stop talking with each other or listening to each other.

Sometimes marriage partners stop talking because they are afraid they will be hurt or will hurt the other. Many spouses at times wonder, "Would he or she still love me if I said what I really felt or thought?" We fear that our partner might not understand or might take offense. A marriage in which partners lack the courage and confidence to talk about things that matter is headed for failure.

We've already acknowledged that most of us begin trying to change the other person soon after we're married. We do battle over the very things for which we chose the other. Yet when we feel the other is out to change us, we react. We rebel in protest.

We feel unacceptable because we are not accepted as we are. Trying to change another drives a wedge into our relationship. It creates tension and crushes the other's ego. If we feel we are not accepted, we find it impossible to love tenderly. Rejection leads to rebellion. It may even destroy love.

Another serious threat to a marriage often comes with the arrival of the first child. The test is whether the wife, and sometimes the husband, will give first attention to the child or to the marriage partner. Will the parent realize that parenthood is passing and that the partnership is permanent?

Will the parents understand that only as they grow in love together as husband and wife will they be able to meet the child's basic needs for warmth, acceptance, security, and love? And if the parents' partnership is not one of growing love, the child will not feel true affection and love, no matter how well she is provided for physically, intellectually, or mentally.

When children come, the danger is that the wife will be more concerned about being a mother than being a mate. And the father may be more concerned about the paycheck than about the partnership. The result is a growing distance between them instead of a growing oneness, which is what they both need to withstand the pressures of parenthood and to support their relationship when the children are grown and gone.

This is the reason the Scriptures stress the kind of relationship husbands and wives should maintain and why they say so little about rearing children. Even in those places where the Scriptures give direction about child guidance, they are preceded by much more extensive instruction on the relationship of husband and wife. Remember: *Partnership is permanent; parenthood is passing. Keep the partnership in good repair and parenting will come much more easily and naturally.*

After the wedding vows, marriage partners too easily forget the common courtesies of life. If they thought consideration, kindness, and words and acts of love were necessary to cultivate their love during courtship, they are just as necessary to maintain and mature their love after they are married.

Dips come into our marriages because we fail to take time for and with each other. Before we were married we found time to see each other, to talk, and to go places together. After marriage, nothing should substitute for time with each other. Money, things, a bigger house or bank account will not substitute for listening, loving, and sharing together.

Some time ago I counseled a couple in their fifties. They told me that their home was a happy one for more than twenty-five years. They had a good relationship; they enjoyed their children. But as their business continued to grow, so did their desire for things. The husband said, "Our trouble really began to be serious when we built our third new house. As the business prospered we built larger. We also found ourselves going different ways. I went with the fellows golfing; my wife went with the women to one club or another. We drifted apart as we found interests too much outside each other." They had become strangers in the same house.

**For further thought:**

> *What unrealistic expectations did you bring to your marriage? Make a list.*

# 11.
# Marks of the After-Marriage Dip

In *Lucky in Love*, Catherine Johnson reports on a survey of couples married from seven years to fifty-five years. A good quarter of them had thought of leaving their spouses. Some, now very happy, had actually packed their bags and gone.

But their marriages had survived and flourished because each was willing to change, make adjustments, and, like mature persons, work on their relationship.

What indicates that a marriage has hit the dip? One of the first signs is that *communication is difficult*. Sometimes it stops entirely. Some couples don't speak for days. Other couples continue to talk, but only about those things they *must* talk about to live in the same house. It is "what" communication: saying what should be done or not be done around the place.

Another indicator of the dip is when *the feeling of love for one's spouse comes and goes*—when some days we feel like we love and other days we feel that we never loved. We may be sure that we can never love again and that our love must not have been genuine in the first place.

In the dip we simply *assume the other is there*. We assume that each will go about one's own responsibility. We simply exist together with neither making the effort to connect to or consider the other.

The dip is *a time of great loneliness.* Differences which we don't understand drive us apart. We feel we have little in common with each other.

*We assume we are incompatible.* We cannot see that the strengths in our mate's opposite temperament can be a great asset. We feel we are so incompatible that we have no hope. We begin to go our separate ways. We communicate only what we must. We stick to our separate corners, doing our own chores or reading our papers and magazines. And our marriage becomes a very lonely arrangement.

A young woman once remarked to me, "At least if I were married, I wouldn't be lonely." I replied, "Some of the loneliest people I've ever met have been married people." There is no loneliness like the loneliness of those who live together yet are growing apart.

The dip is *a period of grave doubts.* We begin to wonder if we might make a better choice if we had the opportunity to start over. We look around and see others who seem happy. Sometimes we wish we had married someone else. We may meet another person at work or socially who is experiencing the same estrangement. We share our loneliness and find ourselves drawn to this new person.

This is the point at which many marriages break up. Usually, though not always, it happens in the first two years of marriage. The largest bulge in the divorce rate today comes during the first two and a half years after the wedding.

This says that couples hit the dip, imagine their love is dead, and give up in divorce. They never realize all the love that is still in store for those who understand what is happening and begin working together to build a happy marriage.

Many see divorce as a solution and blithely enter a new marriage, believing that now they will be understood. The new spouse, however, usually has essentially the same qualities as the first mate. The second marriage will require the understanding and work each partner should have been willing to put into the first marriage.

In the dip, *sexual problems become real.* The husband complains the wife is cold; the wife complains she feels no love. Experienced marriage counselors and well informed physicians increasingly are adopting the view that a couple's sexual relations reflect the health of their entire marital relationship. But they do not determine it.

Dr. Paul Popenoe says: "Without fail, sex problems are solved when a couple does not focus on sex, but on other parts of their relationship: doing things together, respecting each other, enjoying each other, and working with personal faults. As a result, the couple's sexual performance becomes satisfying to both."

**For further thought:**

*What other marks of the after-marriage dip can you list?*

# 12.
# Hope Ahead

Persons in the dip hurt profoundly. They have probably never before felt such deep hurt. It is essential to remember, however, that as long as we hurt, we still care and there is hope. Love is dead when there is no longer any pain.

One of the disturbing things about the dip is that so many persons believe there is no chance for something better. They live in the dip. Many marriage jokes are based on the assumption that marriage is one long drag or dip; that to be married means that one lives at a low level of communication; that one is caught and can't get loose.

Many couples resign themselves to living in the dip. As long as these couples have children growing up and hope to advance economically, they can endure a lot. But we see many twenty-year fractures. The divorce rate bulges again for marriages that are about twenty to twenty-five years old. Why? Has something suddenly happened?

No, nothing has happened suddenly. The couple has lived in the low level of the dip for many years. Now the children they lived for are gone. Often at about age forty-five, persons see little possibility for further advancement in their jobs. The things they lived for when they began giving themselves to things other than their marriages and homes are suddenly gone or on the wane. Husbands or wives often say at that point—in one way or another—"I'm not going to live like this anymore."

In a climate where divorce is widely accepted, and with

far fewer pressures to hold marriages together than in past generations, divorce often follows. But the divorce is not really sudden. These persons have simply not lived for each other for a long time. They hit a dip and never climbed out of it.

Many happy marriages go through at least three stages. The first is *mutual enjoyment,* the honeymoon stage. This is the sheer delight of belonging to each other. The danger here is in expecting our partner to give what only God can give—eternal ecstasy. This is one time to face up to our finiteness. Ruel L. Howe in *Sex and Religion Today* says, "Much marriage difficulty and unhappiness are due to the failure of the partners to accept the fact of their finiteness and its meaning. Instead, they hold themselves up to ideals or performance possible only to God." "Eternal love," says the old proverb, "lasts two years, and immortality five— unless you take care." So marriage needs a second stage.

Stage Two might be called *mutual adjustment.* This is when we begin honestly to face up to differences we never dreamed existed. Now we must learn to live together and love each other in spite of our differences. In courtship, we stress similarities; in marriage, our differences become dramatic. We learn that marriage is not just two people enjoying each other. It is also two people going into partnership, which involves a lot of hard work, planning, and sharing. We come to understand that marriage works only if we make it work. A good marriage is not a gift handed to us at the wedding. It is something we create through long days of toil and effort. We can be side by side but poles apart unless we adjust to each other. A good marriage is a goal to strive after, not a privilege possessed automatically.

Because adjustment can be and usually is painful, many marriages break up as they enter this stage. But if we are mature enough to be determined to progress and grow together, the adjusting process can be a pleasure.

Studies show that the romantic illusion of the courtship and honeymoon usually lasts a year or so at the most. No marriage is soundly built until married love takes the place of romantic illusions. Those who do not move to married love break up. The marks of married love are: an acceptance of each other as he or she is, a desire to make the other happy, an eagerness to work out differences as they surface, a focus on building the marriage rather than one's own ego, a commitment to think in terms of "we" rather than "I," a sense of being companions in a common cause, and progress toward a lifestyle which both want to pursue.

Stage Three in a growing happy marriage could be named *mutual fulfillment.* Now the excitement is different than the honeymoon stage. It is more solid and satisfying.

At this stage we have learned to know each other and to love each other from the depths of our beings. We have a profound sense of belonging to each other. At this stage we have confidence because we have learned to deal with all kinds of problems together. And we are stronger because of this.

Countless persons enter marriage desiring a happiness defined only in courtship terms. In many ways, courtship cannot be a model for marriage. Who could live with that much nervous tension and attention? Deeper love is realized in the peace of partnership and fulfillment.

**For further thought:**
> *Do you know couples who have divorced after twenty to twenty-five years of marriage? What do you think has happened?*

# 13.
# We'd Do It the Same Again

Following the publication of our book *If We Were Starting Our Marriage Again*, Betty and I were sent on two weeks of TV shows across the country—a different city each day. We heard concern expressed everywhere about what is happening to marriages and families. The dramatic increase in divorce, the skyrocketing number of single-parent households, and the effect of both upon children, the ravaging abuse which adults and children are experiencing, as well as the general deterioration of family and social values, were high on the agenda of many who interviewed us.

We soon learned during our discussions on the air, and afterwards, that we were talking with many persons who could not imagine being married to the same person for more than thirty years. It seemed that none were living with their original spouses.

One man expressed frankly what so often happens: "It is my fourth time around, and, crazy me, I married the same kind of woman each time."

Of course he did! Why? Because, although he didn't realize it, he was drawn to persons who had those qualities which he didn't have. He was attracted to persons who had abilities that he lacked. He married opposites because he naturally chose persons who completed him.

When persons divorce and remarry, they almost always marry the same kind of individual because that is the kind of person they need. Unless they understand this and are prepared to make the necessary adjustments to grow together, their second, third, and fourth marriages will be just as unsatisfactory as their first, usually more so.

Many couples who divorce and remarry are frank to admit, in their most honest moments, that it would have probably been much easier to make their first marriages work than to leave their first loves. Beginning all over again was not the clean solution they expected. In "The Odd Couple," two men, unable to live with their wives, decide to live with one another. Each brings the same habits, quirks, and character he brought to his marriage. When the story ends, the men are separating for the same reason they left their wives. Neither was willing to change himself to make a go of the companionship.

### *For further thought:*

> *The United States has more divorce than any other country. What, in your opinion, is the reason? Wrong expectations? Wrong suppositions? Inadequate preparation? Pure selfishness? Other reasons?*

# II.

# Build
## on
# Commitment

# 1.
# *Commitment Is the Key*

Last summer we visited friends who were students with us in seminary. We talked about the direction of our lives since those earlier times together, and about our marriages and families. John and Ellen told us they have repeated their wedding vows to each other at least twice a week since their marriage thirty years ago.

"Twice a week?" we asked.

"Yes," they said, "we memorized our vows to say to each other, so why not say them to each other more than at the wedding?" We knew that some couples repeated their vows at each anniversary, but twice a week! That was new.

As we thought and talked about John and Ellen's practice, we think we discovered their secret of happiness in marriage and life. John and Ellen likely had difficult times, as every couple has. But it was their constant commitment and their concrete reminder of it which helped to pull them through the rough spots and made their journey joyful and enduring.

Jacob and Amanda Friesen live in Mountain Lake, Minnesota. Jacob called one day, inviting me to their home. "Although you may forget me, I guarantee you will never forget my wife," he promised.

Jacob and Amanda were married in 1936. Several years later, all of Amanda's joints were stiffened from rheumatoid arthritis. She was unable to bend her body, and for many years she lay in bed, unable to move more than her lips and eyelids. Jacob and Amanda have lived together with this condition for over forty years. She is able to see persons and read by adjusting her prism glasses. Jacob made a bed for her which uses electric power to turn a gear, so that the bed can move from a horizontal to a vertical position.

During my visit, Jacob and Amanda reflected that it was because of their deep assurance that they married in the will of God, and because of their ongoing commitment to God and to each other, that their relationship has been strong all these years. This deep commitment has helped Jacob be happy, kind, and considerate, ministering to Amanda's need. So also, a deep commitment to God and her husband has kept Amanda loving, happy, and gracious, growing in character, in her interest in many things and persons, and in a ministry of prayer, while her body was immobile.

Jake and Amanda told me that they believe the missing word in much of the discussion about marriage today is "commitment." Out of deep commitment come all the other ingredients which have kept them strong, loving, and faithful.

After all our years of marriage—and of leading marriage retreats and seminars—Betty and I have concluded this: If we were starting our marriage again, we would emphasize and build on commitment even more than we have. We confess that it was our commitment to God and to each other, and our deep sense of what permanence means in marriage, that helped us survive difficult stretches and brought us to a fuller love today.

### For further thought:

*Do you think of certain persons who have the kind of commitment discussed in this chapter? Do you believe that commitment is the key to an enduring marriage?*

# 2.
# Commitment
# to Permanence

"To love someone," says Erich Fromm in *The Art of Loving*, "is not just a strong feeling. It is a decision, it is a judgment, it is a promise." I am persuaded of the value of permanence in marriage and of the teaching that says, "Therefore what God has joined together, let no one separate" (Mark 10:9, NRSV).

Our daughter and her husband wrote their own wedding vows. We were struck with the seriousness with which they took their commitment when they said, "We will not consider divorce as an option." I believe that to do so is to weaken marriage from the start. To consider divorce as an option is to deny the sacredness of marriage that is taught in the Scriptures.

Joseph Bayly writing in *Eternity* magazine said, "Somehow we must restore the sacredness of the marriage vows. Maybe there could be two different ceremonies: one for those who have forsworn divorce and remarriage, and another for those who consider divorce and remarriage an option 'if it doesn't work out.' I'd like to see all the latter such ceremonies relegated to the County Clerk's Office."

In an article entitled "Build on the Dignity of Marriage," Waylon Ward declared, "One of the most significant factors affecting marriage appears to be the idea that *love* becomes the foundation couples try to build on, instead of *commit-*

*ment.* Most couples' understanding of love is emotional and fickle. They fall in love, get married, fall out of love, and get a divorce."

Judson and Mary Landis stress that a commitment to permanence in marriage is the only logical starting point from which a successful marriage can be built. They say in *Building a Successful Marriage* that those who marry considering divorce as possible are already steering toward divorce. Successful cooperation in marriage is impossible when limitations are set upon it. The will to succeed is motivated, many times, by the commitment to permanence.

Without this commitment, small difficulties drive persons apart. All who are married for even a few years know that no meaningful or lasting marriage can be built on the philosophy, "We will live together as long as we love." Rather, marriage can last only on the commitment, "We will love together as long as we live."

> What greater thing is there for two human souls
> Than to feel that they are joined for life—
> To strengthen each other in all labor,
> To rest on each other in all pain,
> To be one with each other in silent, unspeakable
>     memories
> At the moment of the last parting.
> —George Eliot

Richard C. Halverson, former Chaplain of the United States Senate, commented about how this basic commitment deepened intimacy and love between him and his wife. "When the marriage covenant is taken seriously, however troublesome the learning-growing process, difficulties serve to deepen intimacy and mature love. This has been the central reality throughout our increasingly fulfilling, yet not trouble-free, relationship . . ."

Don Augsburger in *Marriages That Work* expressed it this way: "Often in premarital counseling I have wished it were possible to communicate adequately to young people beginning their life together the incalculable blessings available to couples who honor their marriage covenant, no matter how difficult it may seem. The word that comes nearest to identify what I as a husband feel is the word *security*. It is a condition which is the fruit of facing difficulties and misunderstandings together, of learning to request forgiveness, and of forgiving. It is the product of struggle—struggle which deepens intimacy and matures love . . . "

### *For furthur thought:*

> *Do the couples you know who are getting married take the permanency of marriage seriously, or do they consider divorce as an option?*

# 3.
# *Commitment Is Security*

A friend of mine just returned from Europe where he had gone to officiate at a wedding. He told me about the strong statement that is made in a traditional German Christian wedding. "If anyone interferes with this union, the wrath of God will be upon such." This is an effort to further state the tenacious continuity, finality, and seriousness of marriage.

Marriage must have this security for stability and for love to grow. This dependability is essential so that love and understanding can develop with real depth. Those who begin without this point of permanence will find marriage to be quite different than those refuse to think of marriage as a temporary relationship.

When Jesus was asked about the meaning of marriage and whether it can be dissolved, he referred to the original and basic statement about marriage in Genesis 2. This passage is pointed to in every major discussion of marriage in the Scripture. What do we find here?

First, the passage points out the persons in marriage—a man and a woman.

Second, the verses state the primary purpose of marriage. Man and woman are partners who become "one flesh." This speaks of a union of husband and wife, of a unique intimacy involving body, mind, and spirit. It means not only to care for the other as one's own body, but to form the closest of all human relationships, even beyond the parent-child relationship.

Third, this passage addresses the permanence of marriage. When bride and groom join hands, and all present hear the words of Jesus, "What God has joined together, let no one separate," there is the clear reminder, spoken to the whole world, that no one should interfere with this commitment.

The words are also a clear statement against either partner forming a romantic or conjugal attachment to anyone else. Here is a reminder, as well, to mothers and fathers not to meddle in the marriage, and to friends not to interfere or cause any disharmony between the ones covenanting for life together. Marriage means, and I aim to say it in every wedding sermon, that persons have ceased looking for other possible marriage or sex partners.

A Christian view of marriage moves far beyond the legal or social bond of a marital contract. Marriage is a covenant made before God and before members of the Christian family. As such, it is an enduring pledge, an unconditional covenant, and more permanent than any legal requirement, marital contract, or social custom.

A Christian view of marriage is a response to God's intention that marriage is permanent. Beyond this, it calls upon God, not only as a witness, but as the one who joins persons in marriage. This includes the promise by husband and wife to be faithful for life.

Thus, the highest intention unites Christians in marriages. The partnership becomes more than a husband-and-wife-covenant to a permanent relationship of personal intimacy. It means that the marriage relationship is part of one's commitment to God.

To advocate such a covenant of permanency and of commitment to each other and to God may seem strange and even old-fashioned at a time when marriage is taken lightly and divorce is easy to get. But all life and experience, as well as Scripture, tell us that a commitment to permanence is the best and only starting point from which a successful marriage can be built.

Dr. Alfred Kinsey cited 6,000 marital histories and nearly 3,000 divorce histories. It is clear, in his opinion, that there is nothing more important to make marriage meaningful and permanent than for a couple to promise from the start of marriage that their marriage is for life. Recent studies of second marriages show that sixty-five percent fail, and, if children are involved, over seventy-five percent of second marriages do not last.

To enter marriage as a Christian means to have the attitude that we are committing ourselves to each other as long as we both shall live, before God and all our other witnesses.

### For further thought:

*How would you describe what a Christian commitment in marriage is and what it involves?*

# 4.
# *Love Is a Commitment— Not a Feeling*

A relationship that depends upon feelings in order to express love will deteriorate and die.

When our first child was born two years after we were married, our peaceful nights vanished. In fact, all our children wakened us numerous times every night during their first years. We got up at all hours to feed them, not because it felt so good getting up at night and losing sleep, but because love led us to do it.

If we wait for good feelings before we demonstrate love, we will not show our love as often as we ought to. We need to rise above our own preferences out of our concern for our commitment to each other. When we do what love would do, we find that the feelings of love follow our actions.

We now know that love is not so much a feeling as it is a commitment to act in love, to do what love should do in each situation.

A spirit of self-gratification, which says "I must always be me" and asks "What is in it for me?"—rather than "What can I do for you?"—destroys happiness. Self-fufillment cannot be each spouse's primary interest if their marriage is to be happy. Such an attitude destroys the very fabric of truly caring for each other. It characterizes the adolescent who is still searching for independence, rather than the adult who knows the meaning and need of interdependence.

One of the best things we can give children is a deep sense that their parents are committed to each other through thick and thin. A child without this security is at sea and has great difficulty developing the stability needed to cope with life and to build a lasting marriage later in life.

During our children's growing up years, we were separated for days at a time because of work and travel. We often talked together about upcoming separations. Numerous times before these out-of-town trips, one of our children developed high fevers which we could not understand. Finally the doctor diagnosed the problem as "daddy-itis." We decided we'd better take a different approach to such pending separations. We avoided burdening the small child with talk of Daddy's leaving beforehand and tried to spend special times together as a relaxed family. And the fevers stopped.

A wise person wrote words that we ought always to keep before us: "The massed experience of mankind would justify us in saying to any couple who sets out on the career of love, 'Now hold together. Hold together even when the light seems to have gone out and your way looks dark and dull. Hold together even when it hurts.'"

Is love a feeling? Absolutely! But the love which lasts a lifetime is much more than a feeling. It is a love based on the kind of commitment we made in our wedding vows—to live together as long as we live, and not to live together only as long as we love.

### For further thought:

*What do you understand the difference to be between love as a commitment and love as a feeling?*

# 5.

# *The Blessing of Commitment*

Some years ago anthropologist Margaret Mead stated frankly, "The most serious thing that is happening . . . is that people enter marriage with the idea that it is terminable." This attitude stands in the way of working at problems which every marriage faces.

The depth of the commitment we make to each other is what holds our marriages together during the difficult days. If that commitment is to permanence, then it will not be superseded by financial, health, or any other problems a marriage may face. When our commitment to each other is greater than our problems, the problems can be solved or endured. But if our commitment is weak, then even small difficulties, discouragements, and disillusionments will drive us apart. If the commitment is weak, we will not work at our problems.

Just because the going gets difficult at times does not mean the marriage is doomed. Newlyweds, in the haze of romance and glamour, worry that their first quarrel has ruined their marriage. It could, in fact, be the beginning of a unity achieved only by struggle, tears, and talking together.

The happiest marriages are not those with the fewest problems, but those in which the partners pledge to work at their problems together, knowing that commitment to each other is greater than any problem. If commitment to each other remains strong, no sickness can shake love's hold, no ill fortune can destroy love's foundation, no hard times can snuff out love's spirit and strong support, and no separation can diminish love's noble steadfastness and unswerving fidelity.

One of the best definitions of love comes from someone who has been married for many years: "Love is what you've been through together." Just as a diamond is nothing but pieces of black coal welded together under terrific pressure, deep married love is that most precious possession which increases in value with every day and year of pulling and sticking together.

Dr. Richard C. Cabot wrote, "Perhaps the greatest blessing in marriage is that it lasts so long . . . Out of many shared years, one life. In a series of temporary relationships, one misses the ripening, gathering, harvesting, joys, the deep, hard-won truths of marriage."

It takes a lifetime of love and loyalty to begin understanding the depth and satisfaction which God intended for those who commit themselves until "death do us part."

**For further thought:**
> *What helps you keep your commitment strong?*
> *What blessings of commitment have you found?*

# III.

# Continue
# the
# Courtship

# 1.

# *The Romance Continues*

William Jennings Bryan was posing for a portrait. The painter asked him, "Why do you wear your hair so long?"

Bryan replied, "When I was courting Mrs. Bryan, she objected to the way my ears stood out, and, so to please her, I let my hair grow over them."

"But," said the artist, "that was many years ago. Don't you think you should have your hair cut now?"

"Why?" asked Bryan in astonishment. "The romance is still going on!"

Love that lasts is not the love that led us to the altar, but the love we express and experience each day. If kindness, courtesy, consideration, and words and acts of love were necessary to nurture our love while we were dating, these same attitudes and behavior are just as necessary for our married love to mature and be maintained.

Most of us have learned that when we practice even a few of the courtesies and kindnesses we remembered to do before we were married, our marriage benefits immensely. Special little gifts, kisses on meeting and leaving, the words "I love you" and "Thank you"—all keep a marriage from growing dull.

On the other hand, we eventually realize that no matter how good our marriage was at the start, it will not blossom in beauty and blessing if we leave out the very things which built love in the first place. We soon discover that if we miss opportunities to show and share love, it fades and can be nearly lost.

Shakespeare wrote:

> They do not love
> that do not show their love.

I believe that we do not grow in love if we do not speak and share our love. Sometimes we need to learn to love all over again. We need to renew and continue our courtship.

· Charles L. Allen in his slender and delightful book *The Miracle of Love* tells of a man who had a peculiar habit. Each week he came home from work, showered, and put on good clothes. Then he went out, got into the car, and left.

In a short time he returned, went to the house, and rang the doorbell. His wife greeted him at the door. They sat and talked for a while in the living room, then went out for dinner and entertainment. When they came home he drove to the front of the house, escorted his wife to the door, and gave her a good-night kiss. Then he put the car in the garage and came in the back door.

Pure sentiment, you say? After talking with those about to be married and those who are married for many years, I believe we need much less sentiment before marriage and a lot more sentiment after marriage.

After counseling couples for many years, I am almost ready to promise—perhaps even guarantee—that your marriage will go on gloriously if you continue to do just fifty percent of the kindnesses you practiced before marriage. Some couples look at me strangely and I repeat the guarantee. Of course, at this point, engaged couples have no problem practicing these courtesies. But those of us who are married know how easy it is to let the very things which build love go by the wayside after we are married.

We are as slow to catch on at times as the old codger who took his wife to the doctor because she was depressed.

After only a few minutes in the office the doctor came out and said, "Sir, I want you to come in, too."

"I want to tell you," the doctor said, "what your wife needs. Your wife needs a loving hug and kiss at least three times a week."

The old-timer thought for several moments and said, "Well, doctor, I think I could bring her in for that Monday and Wednesday, but I can't make it Friday."

One major reason why many marriages move to the mediocre and lose meaning is that the partners forget or refuse to practice the little things which build love.

### For further thought:

*How do you feel about the guarantee that if fifty percent of the common courtesies you practiced before you were married were to continue, your marriage would go on gloriously?*

# 2.
## *Staying in Love*

I was invited for a meal by a couple who were my classmates in college. Their children were in their late teens and early twenties. Their only daughter was present, along with the young man she was soon to marry.

Out of the corner of my eye I noticed during the meal that the young couple joined hands at times. When she spoke, he looked into her eyes. Several times one reached out to touch the other's shoulder, responding affectionately to each other as they spoke.

When they moved from the table to the window, they kissed and smiled warmly to each other. And in the kitchen they talked and laughed the whole time they washed the dishes together. They were living for each other.

Few if any marriages would dry up if even a small part of the sentiment expressed before marriage were continued after marriage. Marriage would not only survive, but would sparkle with satisfaction and happiness.

Marriage counselor Jerome Folkman proposes this formula for a successful marriage: Have the wedding and then forget it. "Just act like you are not married at all. Keep right on being lovers."

In *Lovers in Marriage*, Lewis Evely says the first obligation of a married couple is "to be alive." He says that few of us consider this obligation. In Evely's words, "A home is not destroyed by quarrels, by unforeseen difficulties, by money crises, or even by infidelity. What destroys a home is the rut of routine. When, without realizing it, you stop looking at each other, or talking with each other, or quarreling with each other, then the marriage is in danger."

Staying in love involves many things. It involves planning time together. We did it before we were married and we assumed we would have all the time in the world after we got married. Yet the number one complaint, particularly of married women, is that, "We don't have enough time together." To love is to help each other grow by intentionally hearing, understanding, and reinforcing each other. It is putting a premium on communication.

Part of cultivating love for one's spouse is to continue to stay physically attractive to each other. I need to see my partner as a person of beauty. Yes, we stress the primariness of inner beauty, but at the same time, as we did before we were married, we need to be alert to our appearance. We each need to guard and enhance the attractiveness of spirit and appearance which first captured the attention and approval of our spouse.

It is disappointing when a husband and wife become careless about their clothing, or their weight, or their cleanliness. Personal neatness and hygiene are part of what makes a person attractive and are just as important after marriage as before.

Courtesy also conveys our love. Countess Clarita de Forceville said, "If love is the foundation of a happy marriage, good manners are its walls and roof." Courtesy cultivates respect and love; courtesy unites people and brings an agreeable and caring tone to a home. Marriage is a friendship, and it thrives on the exquisite care that courtesy encourages.

A marriage that has no time for courtesy will fall into rudeness. A marriage that has no time for compliments will have time for complaints. A marriage that has no time for kind, loving words will find time for harsh, critical words.

Henry Drummond's definition of courtesy is "Love in little things." Love says "please" because that acknowledges respect for the other person. Love says "Thank you" because that expresses gratitude for the other person. Love says "Pardon me" because that request recognizes the dignity of the other person.

Love extends and accepts small kindnesses, because it knows the need for interdependence. Without courtesy, love loses its grand beauty. Married love blossoms when it is cultivated with appreciation. The closer a relationship, the more pain one can inflict with a look, tone, gesture, or word of thoughtlessness—and the more dignity one can grant by gracious words and actions.

**For further thought:**
> *What would you list as the top five things that are necessary to stay in love?*

# 3.

# *Love—*
# *Its Character and Conduct*

John A. Redhead, Jr. told about a married couple he once visited. "An atmosphere of gloom was so heavy in the place you could cut it with a knife. The husband and wife told me, 'We're having a hard time getting along, and we wanted to see if you could help us.' I sensed immediately that the situation was beyond me, so I sent a little prayer for wiser wisdom, and God did not let me down. Never before had I thought of Paul's words on love in connection with marriage. I asked for a Bible and turned to First Corinthians, the thirteenth chapter and read.

"The words spoke for themselves, and the husband and wife seemed to truly hear them. In that passage they found a mirror for themselves and were able to see how and why they were failing. We bowed in prayer together, asking God to give us more of that kind of love, and then I left. The last time I saw these folks they were together and they were smiling. These words from First Corinthians are the best description I know anywhere of Christian married love, and our business now is to think about what they have to say to us."

Here in a swift summary are fifteen terms which describe the character and conduct of true love. I include nothing here about feelings, because love is first of all a way of responding to other people. If First Corinthians 13 were put into practice, little, if anything else, would be needed to make a happy marriage.

LOVE IS PATIENT. Patience is priceless. Many of our unhappy experiences come from our own or other's impatient words and behavior. Gerald Kennedy says, "As one grows older, one comes to the conclusion that more lives are destroyed by impatience than any other sin."

Patience makes us willing to suffer long rather than cause suffering to another. Just like we want others to be patient with us, we can learn to be patient with another's faults. Patience makes it possible for us to refrain from saying something harsh or acting hastily.

LOVE IS KIND. Kindness means being aware of how the other feels, considering those feelings, and responding in a way which helps the other feel better. Joseph Joubert points out that "a part of kindness consists of loving people more than they deserve." Kindness is love in little things. It is thinking of others and speaking of others in the most helpful way.

In the book of Proverbs, a godly wife and mother is praised because, "In her tongue is the law of kindness."

Beth Robertson wrote a beautiful little verse:

> When I think of the charming people I know,
> It's surprising how often I find
> The chief of the qualities that make them so
> Is just that they are kind.

LOVE IS NOT JEALOUS. At its root, jealousy is selfishness, and since true love is not selfish, it is not jealous. Love does not covet the praise or position which goes to someone else. Since love is not looking for center stage, but instead is looking out for the welfare of the other, it has no reason to be jealous.

LOVE IS NOT BOASTFUL. Love does not show off its own goodness or greatness. It does not go on parade or put on airs. Love sees the good qualities in the other and speaks of them, rather than boasting of its own accomplishments. Love does not say, "Look what I did."

LOVE IS COURTEOUS. It is surprising how soon after marriage we allow ourselves to be rude to each other. True love is courteous and treats the other as important and worthy of the most gracious behavior. Such love says "thank you" and "please" as consistently to one's close family members, as to one's co-workers or business associates or friends.

LOVE DOES NOT SEEK ITS OWN. Love is unselfish and does not insist on its own way. Those who are still putting themselves first are really not ready for marriage. Love takes us on a different path. It does not talk about its "rights." Instead, it wants to help the other person realize her or his delights. In accomplishing that, one finds one's own true fulfillment.

LOVE IS NOT IRRITABLE. Love is not touchy, nor does it keep a record of injuries or insults. Henry Drummond in *Pax Vobiscum* says, "There is a disease called 'touchiness'—a disease which, in spite of its innocent name, is one of the greatest sowers of restlessness in the world. Touchiness, when it becomes chronic, is a morbid condition of the inner disposition. It is self-love inflamed to an acute point."

LOVE THINKS NO EVIL. A suspicious person who imagines the worst brings trouble to any relationship. Love believes the best and refuses to believe rumors. And in believing the best, love draws the best from the one who is loved, as well as the one loving.

LOVE REJOICES IN THE TRUTH. Love is happy when truth prevails, when wrongs are righted, and when relationships are restored. Love refuses to repeat wrongs; instead, it enjoys pointing out the good in other persons and situations.

LOVE BEARS ALL THINGS. Love shows its true character when it bends beneath the load during difficult times and helps bear the trouble, rather than pointing out blame or joining in criticism. But more than that, love is willing to overlook the weakness, failings, and wrongs of another and is even willing to help bear them with the other person.

LOVE BELIEVES ALL THINGS. Love assumes the highest intention from the other person's motives, even when the other's conduct is difficult to understand. Love is trusting.

LOVE HOPES ALL THINGS. Love continues to believe in someone when all others doubt. Love always sees possibilities in persons and has ways of restoring hope to the person who has failed. Love always makes it easy to return.

LOVE ENDURES ALL THINGS. There is no end to love's endurance. Others may give up, but love continues to stand firm. No matter how dark the night, love looks for the dawn and possibilities. True love never does fail. It never lets us down. Would a marriage fail if the couple lived by love's standards? Suppose each of us were always to ask, "What would love do?" The love that is shown in the Scripture— agape love—is not a feeling but a response. True love always seeks to discover what love would do in each experience of life.

### For further thought:

*Do you agree that love is something we can determine to do? What are some of the implications of this?*

# 4.
# *Beware of Narcissism*

Greek mythology tells of a handsome young man named Narcissus. One day he saw his reflection in a still pool of water. He became so infatuated with himself that he could not stop admiring his own face.

From this tale comes the term "narcissistic." It refers to any extreme self-centeredness. *Time* magazine once offered this opinion: "One difficulty in diagnosing pathological narcissism is that the whole culture has turned in a narcissistic direction." We remember the popular best-seller—*Looking Out for #1*. Its basic thesis? "You have to spend time concentrating on making yourself happy."

This narcissistic obsession with self-fulfillment and self-satisfaction has carried over into marriage where husbands and wives each look out for Number One. The attitude wreaks havoc. A happy marriage is impossible alongside such egocentricity. It is no surprise that in many places, the number of divorces now equals or exceeds the number of marriages in a given year.

Marriage counselor Waylong Ward writes, "It is self-centeredness that causes each mate to take care of self first and to be insensitive to the partner and marriage commitment.

"I have been involved with hundreds of couples during the past seven years as a therapist, a group leader, and conference leader. I've met most major marital problems with those couples at one time or another. As I look at marriages today, one issue seems to be of greater importance than any other. It affects all aspects of our culture—and not just marital relationships. This selfish individuality is demonstrated continually in our world by persons demanding that their needs be met, whether it be tossing trash from their cars or satisfying their personal appetites, regardless of what effect such gratifications might have on other people. 'I have the right . . . ' is the slogan of this narcissistic epidemic."

Ward points out that much personal concern is turned inward. The slogans of much of our society are "I must be me," "Self-fulfillment," "Do your own thing," "Take care of Number One," "What's in it for me?" and "Self-actualization." Even in religious life, questions tend to center on, "What can Jesus and the church do for me?"

From "Springs of Indian Wisdom" come these words:

> The sun and the moon
> Are not mirrored in cloudy waters,
> Thus the Almighty cannot be mirrored
> In a heart that is obsessed by
> "Me and Mine."

Another says it succinctly: "The key reason why the American family is in trouble is that too many American husbands and wives consider their families to be of secondary importance. Their number one priority is themselves, their personal growth, fulfillment, and all the other things we say when what we mean is: Me first."

The real purpose of marriage is mutual fulfillment. Both partners have needs. The first key to a happy relationship is what you put into it. What you get out of it is secondary. The approach of Jesus still works: "Give and it shall be given to you."

A survey of couples married over fifty years reveals some interesting findings. To the question: "To what do you attribute your long and happy marriage?", not one responded, "I had to look out for myself." Not one said, "I had to be concerned with my own development." Not one mentioned independence or even self-actualization.

How did they answer? They spoke of commitment to each other and to their marriages, in spite of difficulties. Repeatedly they said, "We tried to live for each other" and "We tried to put the other first."

E. Stanley Jones wrote, "Yourself in your own hands is a problem and a pain; yourself in the hands of God is a possibility and a power."

Marriage flourishes when partners commit to fulfill the needs of the other. Of course we cannot fulfill each other's needs fully. But we can know happiness when we commit ourselves to do what we can to make our spouse both satisfied and content. Henry Drummond said, "There is no happiness in having or getting, but only in giving."

The Scripture, as strange as it may sound in our narcissistic age, is still the way to true happiness—"Love is not selfish," and "Think of the other better than yourself."

**For further thought:**
> *Do you consider the present time to be more narcissistic than a generation or so ago? Why or why not?*

# 5
# Learn to Love Again and Again

According to a German medical magazine reporting the results of an insurance company survey, a husband who kisses his wife each day before they separate for work will probably live five years longer, earn twenty percent more money, lose up to fifty percent less time because of illness, and be involved in fewer automobile accidents than the husband who doesn't kiss his wife each day.

My wife Betty heard me tell this story. A day or so later I was hurrying out of the house. Betty came running after me. "What do you want?" I asked. She threw her arms around me and gave me a big kiss as she said, "I want you to live longer."

We have found that marriage ebbs and flows. In every marriage there are times of special closeness, as well as times of tension and distance. It is unrealistic to expect a marriage to continue on one high emotional level, to be a continual panacea for trouble. Real life is not like that. The important thing is to learn how to deal with the lows as well as the highs.

Too often we are tempted to be escapist. When difficulty comes, we think immediately about how to get out, rather than concentrating on how to cope with the situation. Our mood today is geared toward evading every discomfort. We take pills to prevent every kind of pain. We have forgotten that pain can produce perception and courage, as well as a caring and compassionate spirit.

Through the low times of our marriage, we have found it possible to love all over again. That is because love is not a shot in the arm which, having once received it, guarantees that we will live happily ever after. It is not a bolt of lightning out of the blue which hits us and then stays with us forever. It is not an arrow which Cupid shoots and we need only receive. Love is learned.

In marriage counseling I see couples who tell me that there is nothing left in their marriages. They no longer have any feeling of love for each other—every drop of love is drained away, they say. The only alternative they see is divorce. And they want my sanction to separate.

To such couples I simply say, "You did love each other one time, didn't you?"

"Yes!" they reply. "We did love, but it's all over. Our love is dead."

"Then there is only one thing you can do," I tell them. (Here the couple expects me to say that their marriage is done and the only answer is divorce.) Imagine their surprise when I tell them, "The only thing you can do is to learn to love all over again."

"Learn to love again?" they ask in shocked response. "How can we do that?"

"You learn to love again in exactly the same way you did in the first place," I answer. "By doing and saying and practicing those things which built love in the beginning. Just continue the courtship."

"Our marriage was on the rocks," wrote a woman. "I did not love Robert. Then I began to ask, 'How would I act if I did love my husband?' I consciously began learning his likes and dislikes. I prepared his favorite dishes. I joined in his hobbies. I bought surprises to put in his lunch. I gave him my love on every occasion possible. Now I love him with all my heart.

"My greatest reward came the other day when our teenager said, 'Mom, I'm lucky.' 'Oh,' I replied. 'Why?' 'Because you and dad love each other. You'd be surprised how many kids have parents who fight and quarrel most of the time.'"

Love is often as much the fruit of marriage as it is the root of marriage. George E. Sweazey writes in his book *In Holy Marriage*, "Marriage is not the result of love; it is the opportunity to love. People marry so they may find out what love is. It is not destiny that makes a person the one true love; it is life. It is the hardships that have been faced together. It is bending over sickbeds and struggling over budgets; it is a thousand good-night kisses and good-morning smiles; it is vacations at the seashore and conversations in the dark; it is growing reverence for each other which comes out of esteem and love."

**For further thought:**

> *Why do you think couples are often ready to give up their marriages?*

# 6.

## Children Reap the Benefits

Children are blessed by parents who are happy with each other and who demonstrate their love for each other. A friend of ours who is a teacher in Canada asked his class of first-graders before Father's Day, "What is a dad and why do you love yours?"

Among the many intriguing responses was this one: "A dad is a father and a boyfriend; my mom's boyfriend. I love him because he hugs and kisses me. My mom likes my daddy, too." Happy the child who has such a sense of love between mother and father. When this kind of love is present, the child will benefit enormously. But when love between parents is not known, seen, or felt, it is nearly impossible for children to make up for its absence in any way.

Psychiatrist Justin S. Green said, "In my twenty-five years of practice, I have yet to see a serious emotional problem in a child whose parents loved each other and whose love for the child was an outgrowth of their love for each other."

When I reflect on my own experiences of closeness, I realize how much these affected all my relationships. Our children felt delight and our love for them when they sensed our love for each other as husband and wife. They loved to join us for a walk as we hooked hands with each other. As they entered their teens, they sometimes said, "Mother and Dad, we want you to go out this evening for a good time together. We'll take care of things here." And we realized all over again that when they saw and sensed our love for each other as their parents, they felt the warmth and wonder in their own spirits.

To this day our children remember in detail the time they said, "Dad, we have a plan. We want you to go to the upstairs phone and call Mother in the kitchen. We want you to make a date with her for the sweetheart banquet next month." They still talk about the excitement they felt as they listened to the conversation between us and as they helped us each choose what we should wear for the special occasion.

### For further thought:

*Can you recall specific times and experiences in your past when you felt love between your parents? What did those occasions do for you?*

# 7.

# *Fresh Discoveries*

Yes, if we were starting our marriage again, we would continue our courtship. Just as we did while we were dating, we would treat our relationship as the most important thing in our lives—one great adventure together. We now know that the time we spend together doing things which express love are not lost times, but moments which multiply all that's good in life.

We now know that when we have romantic fun, we enrich our feelings of love. When we cultivate common interests and enjoy them together, they bind us in bonds of love. We now know that when our children see us as lovers, our relationship with them is at its best. We now realize that only as our children see our deep love for each other can they understand the meaning of true love—and eventually the meaning of God's love.

We recognize now that as we continue our courtship, we continually make fresh discoveries about each other's lives and personalities. No diamond can compare to the sudden bracing realization that we care deeply for each other. Sometimes we learn this through a crisis.

A friend of ours told us how insecure he felt early in his marriage. He sometimes felt very unsure about his wife's love for him. Late one evening he was working in the basement with an arc welder. Suddenly the welder hit an electric wire, causing a loud noise and a flash of light. All the electricity went off. In the dark, he rushed to the garage to check the fuse box.

When he returned, he found his wife sitting on the basement steps crying desperately. She had run to the basement upon hearing the loud noise, found it dark, called her husband—and got no answer. "At that moment," he said, "I did not doubt my wife's love for me. And I haven't doubted it since."

No gem is as precious as loving kindness, a compliment, a smile, a forgiving spirit, or voluntary helpfulness. The happiest partner is not the one who married the best person, but the one who is able to bring out the best in the person he or she married.

All of us feel good about ourselves when we are affirmed. Likewise, we feel good about our relationships when we affirm and compliment each other. When we're told, "You look good in that suit" or "That dress really makes you look fine," we dress in that same outfit again and again. Betty says she still remembers when I told her, "I'm glad you've taken care of yourself. You were the most attractive woman at the banquet tonight. Your eyes sparkle and your face lights up when you converse with people."

I remember that during a discouraging time in my work, Betty gave me a boost that I really needed: "John, I know you don't realize the tremendous confidence a lot of people have in you." I needed that word of assurance. And who should be able to give it better than a loving wife or husband?

In our marriage, a compliment given at the right moment often kept us from discouragement and even despair.

When we commit ourselves to each other's happiness, we multiply happiness. When we commit ourselves to say and do loving things, we are blessed many times over.

When we commit ourselves to respect each other, we make each other respectable; when we honor each other, we make each other honorable. And when we forget ourselves in love for each other, we make each other lovely.

### For further thought:
> *What could you as a couple do to grow in love? Be specific about things you are willing to commit yourselves to.*

# IV.

# *Take Time Together*

# 1.
## *Love Is Spelled TIME*

A severe windstorm swept through Kansas. One couple had their house roof blown off. In addition, so the story goes, the wind lifted the bed in which they were sleeping, dropping it down gently in the barnyard. The wife was whimpering. The husband, in an effort to console his wife, said, "Don't cry! Don't be sad! We'll manage somehow to get everything fixed up." His wife replied, "But I'm not crying because I'm sad. I'm crying because I'm so glad. It's the first time we've been out together in twenty years."

Love is spelled TIME! Love is time together—to be with each other, to do things together and for each other, to relax in each other's presence.

We have often been separated through the years because of my work which required travel. During many months we were apart from each other for more than half the time. When we were together, we tried to build quality time, but that in itself was not enough. Every couple needs special, regular times to discuss special concerns, especially those matters that are bothering them. Unless we find that time regularly, small things will become tremendous trifles which tear at our marriage. It is easy to become strangers within the same family.

Some years ago we were separated for a long period of time. When we were reunited, we made a list of ten things we needed to discuss. They all had to do with our relationship as husband and wife.

Over the course of several days we each wrote our thoughts or concerns or problems in each area. We wrote not only what we were thinking, but also what we were feeling, and we each tried to make as full a statement as possible about each subject. Then we took a day off together and read to each other what we had written. After each subject we talked about our feelings, understandings, disagreements, and the adjustments we felt we needed to make. When we were satisfied, we moved on to the next area.

We will never forget that experience, as well as other similar ones which helped clear up our feelings about ourselves and each other.

We have also regularly taken several days in a cabin in the mountains to renew our relationship. Our pattern is to work on projects or problems in the mornings and then to hike together in the afternoons.

Before we were married we spent as much time together as possible. Somehow we knew our relationship could not grow or even exist, nor could our understandings of each other increase, without regular time together.

We discovered that after marriage a strange thing happened. We assumed that now we were together and that we would be together always. Consequently, we didn't plan for time together. But we weren't automatically together, just because we were married! After marriage we found that we tended to go our own ways. Often the only moments we had together were those in which we were tired or irritated. The best time of day was too often given to going elsewhere and doing things separately.

No wonder a marriage dries up. A happy marriage cannot exist on the crumbs or leftover scraps of time. A good marriage cannot develop on tired time, which is what we usually have when we finally get home, all worn out.

Meaningful communication, so essential to marriage, deteriorates when it is left for hurried, late times. Without great care, prime time is taken over by less important programs which push their way into every marriage.

Further, love has a longing within itself to grow larger and more beautiful. Love does not remain the same. The love of the teens is different from the love of the twenties. And the love of the twenties is different from the love of the thirties. We are constantly changing, so we need time together to stay acquainted with our best friend.

Being married and living in the same house does not guarantee anything. It certainly does not guarantee that we will not be lonely or that we will learn to know each other better. Some of the loneliest people each of us knows are married people.

We learn to know each other and experience togetherness when we take time to share each other's souls, to read each other's minds, and to enjoy each other's pleasures and presence.

### For further thought:

> *Why do you think many couples seem to spend less and less vital time together after they are married?*

# 2.

# *A Covenant of Time*

I've heard the excuse, and used the excuse myself early in our family life, that it is not the quantity of time that is important, but the quality of time. That is true, but it is only partially true. Lewis P. Bird is right, I believe: "Courtship days would never have tolerated this cliché, nor will a dynamic family life."

While the slogan has become gospel to many professionals too busy to spend necessary time at home, it is often merely rationalization. The argument keeps us from eliminating committee meetings, church activities, nights at the office, and other competing demands, rather than spending more time with our families.

Sharing dreams, stresses, schedules, questions, memories, and future plans takes time. When we sacrifice quantity of time for quality in family relationships, we usually lose both, and we disappoint those we love who need us to be there and to care.

Over and over again, couples who are married only six months tell me that one of their major problems is that they don't have enough time together. Already they are getting into a routine which robs them of the time they need to build their marriage. And unless they take special pains to correct what is happening, the routine will become a rut and ruin their marriage.

Somehow we find time together before we are married because we know we need time to get to know and enjoy each other. After marriage we get busy with many things and tend to assume that our love will just continue to stay warm and grow.

If we want our marriages to be maturing, caring, growing love relationships, we will need to invest time in them. We will need to commit ourselves to spending time together each day and to giving time to each other to renew our sense of love and togetherness. From the start of marriage we need this covenant. Emergencies will come, but in spite of them, we need to rigorously guard our time together.

When I counsel couples before and after marriage, I talk with them about time. I believe that if we do not take loving, relaxed time together, we will soon be caught in angry, hostile, suspicious time. Studies show clearly that spouses who refuse to allow work to rob them of time with their partner and children accomplish much more at their jobs in both quality and quantity, than spouses who spend much overtime away from home. In fact, we are told that having relaxed, free, and easy access to the people we love decreases our chances of fouling up on the job.

Time is required for building good relationships. When our marriage is a good relationship, the benefits and blessings overflow to every other relationship and responsibility we have. One of the earmarks of a deteriorating marital life is the increasing amount of time spouses spend apart from each other.

We must continually look at and assess those things for which we use our time. Extra work, hours watching TV, shopping, evening meetings, business trips, and a multitude of intrusions all squeeze our time. If we do not scrutinize and sift through these many activities and commitments, we will find ourselves living in a different world from our spouse, and losing what we longed for when we got married—time together.

Make the most of special times. Birthdays, anniversaries, Christmas, Easter, and other holidays are great togetherness-builders. Feelings of warmth and love flow from shared emotions and happiness as we celebrate these seasons. Having dinners and evenings out together help husbands and wives cherish each other.

Attending church, reading the Bible, and praying together all build intimacy. But even with the best intentions, we may let these more routine practices slip by, if we are not committed to them and if we fail to put them into our regular schedules.

Informal, unplanned, ordinary times—often a natural part of family life unless we crowd them out—can richly build our daily love and friendship. There is a reason why so many playwrights have centered dramatic main scenes around the dinner table. Here, while people talk and eat, feelings of belonging and togetherness can grow. Pity the couple and family who do not make much of meal times together.

As couples we ought to cultivate hobbies, projects, and play which we can do together on a regular basis. While it is true that the family that prays together stays together, it is also true that "The family—and the couple—that plays together stays together."

When we take time to be together, we find that the times we are apart have greater meaning.

**For further thought:**
> *Do you think it is necessary to have both quantity and quality time together?*

# 3.
# Check Priorities

One of my good friends said the other day, "One thing Jim has brought to our marriage is that he puts family before his work. He loves his work and has a lot to do, but he knows when to lay his work aside and take time with me and the children." Do you know what else? Jim is also a very good schoolteacher.

Jim can be good everywhere because he keeps his marriage in strong repair. A person who is happy at home is usually a responsible employee. I know, also, that Jim and his family have time for all kinds of service to others. Somehow when we put our family in its proper place, we have more time for God and also for work and service. Wayne Oats said, "Surprisingly enough, finding time for each other ordinarily increases rather than decreases our efficiency at the very tasks that we use as excuses for not finding time."

Thomas W. Klewin, after discussing the all too common pattern of giving our best energies to others and using what is left over for our spouse, wrote, "While dating we save the best of our emotions, feelings, and even physical alertness for each other. And so we ask ourselves, why shouldn't we do the same now that we have actually grown closer to each other through our marriage?"

I find that I must check my priorities again and again. What is most important? My priorities shape and ultimately determine how I use my time, the person with whom I use it, and the kind of benefits I expect to receive from what I do.

Many of us have three main categories of commitments. The first is our loyalty to God. When we put God first, our intimate relationships are almost always blessed. The second claim on our lives is family. And the third claim is work.

Only when we place work after family will our family relationships be right. Only then will our work have a chance of being satisfying and successful. When work prospers and our family falls apart, work also suddenly loses its meaning. When things are in good shape at home, work has a good chance of going well.

Our marriage relationship, I believe, must be second only to our commitment to God. We know that if we are to have time together, we need to *plan* time together. Each of us has the same number of hours in a week. Like a financial budget around which we plan our spending, we may want to institute a time budget around which we plan what is important. Suppose we budget sixty hours for work and travel to and from work each week. Suppose we budget fifty-six hours for sleep. That still leaves forty-two hours to spend on other things. How will we use these hours? Without some planning and thought, we will waste many of them. Without careful planning, we will spend that time doing just about anything except being with our families. If we are to have time together—we need to plan our time.

### For further thought:
*Do you agree with this order of priorities—God, family, work? What are your top five priorities in regard to time?*

# 4.
## Beware of the Thieves

A pastor friend of mine was very busy in church work. He dutifully took time to listen to everyone else's needs and gradually neglected time with his wife. She pleaded over the years that they set aside time for themselves.

Finally one day she was fed up with their relationship and left her husband. Shocked, the pastor husband came for help. In the counseling sessions he heard, for the first time in years, his wife angrily state her feelings and frustrations. She observed that her husband had time for his work and for other people, but had none for her. She was through with their marriage.

But something happened in the next weeks. The man called his wife and made a date to go out together. After a relaxed evening, both felt a new exhilaration. She called me to express her surprise at her husband's action and what it meant to her.

The next week they planned a three-day trip together. Getting away from it all together did wonders. For those days they practiced Dr. Ed Wheat's equation for building love. He calls it the BEST formula—Bless each other in some way every day; Edify or encourage each other in something every day; Spend time together every day; and Touch each other every day. It sounds simple, and it works miracles.

Today that couple is happy again. They learned the hard way that love is spelled TIME.

Charlie Shedd and his wife Martha have a covenant of time. It consists of two parts. They spend at least fifteen minutes a day together, talking about what is happening inside Martha and Charlie. Then, once a week, they take an evening out alone. What they find is that the more time they spend together, the more they want to spend time together.

Many marriages would never take place if persons were as careless about their time together *before* marriage as they are *after* marriage. One of the major reasons for persons drifting apart after they are married is that they imagine their love can grow and their marriage will last without definitely committing themselves to regular and special times together.

Beware of the robbers who steal your time—robbers as real as any who might knock in the back door and steal your valuables. Television is a robber. It takes away precious hours of togetherness. Golf dates, all kinds of evening meetings, sports events, and breakfast meetings can also steal time from our families. Since we plan for all these, we should also plan for time with each other.

Such planning is a sign that we have grown up and that we have outgrown adolescence—which is characterized by conforming to the pressures of the gang, friends, and outside activities. Part of growing up is assigning second place to certain people and projects so we can keep the greater commitment we have made to each other.

This may mean planning a meal away together each week. It may mean setting a definite time each day for talking to each other. The secret is to find little bits of time regularly, rather than to wait for the big vacation or a whole free day in which to do something together.

Even a half hour or less is better than nothing, and it is a lot less complicated and expensive than spending time later in a psychiatrist's or lawyer's office. Betty and I like activities as simple as a mile-long walk around the neighborhood on a summer evening, or a drive into the country or to a park. It's not only refreshing, it is time when we can converse in private.

Several weeks ago we noticed our car wasn't working right. Because we were busy, we didn't get it checked. We knew we needed to take it to the garage but kept putting it off. Then one morning the car didn't start. Finally, with a lot of time and work, we took the car to the garage and had it repaired. The trouble at the start was a simple thing which could have been remedied in a few minutes, had we seen to it immediately. Unattended to, it caused other mechanical problems, plus more inconvenience and poorly used time.

How like marriage that experience was. When we let little things go because we think we don't have time to talk about them and repair them, they become serious and affect our entire relationship. Because we don't take the time early enough, major repairs are sometimes needed.

Before we were married, we planned time to do all kinds of things and go all kinds of places together. And we planned time just to be together—alone. If we plan to do the same now in marriage, we will find love growing in fresh and fulfilling ways. Taking special times away, a day or two together, can also do wonders for a relationship.

Periodically we need serious time to talk about what is happening to us and to listen to the deep concerns each of us has. We need fun times together, too. The family or couple who doesn't have play times is missing out on many good memories.

We have learned that the more time we take with each other, the more we cherish each other, especially if those times have included fun, caring, and conversation. One college study reported that "nothing is more apt to smooth the course of love than communication: the level of marital satisfaction appeared to be related to the amount of time each day a couple spent talking together."

By guarding our regular times together, we have also discovered that when we do need to be separated, we have wonderful memories to think about, and we anticipate being together again, soon.

**For further thought:**

    *What thieves rob you of time together?*

# 5.
## Nourish the Family

Children are blessed when their parents take time to be together. Children of all ages feel close to a mom and dad who have time for each other. You can see it in a little two-year-old who snuggles in between her parents on the sofa. Children want their parents to express love for each other. As our own children got older, they urged us to sit beside each other rather than having them split us up.

Somehow both the smallest child and the growing adolescent feel their mother and dad have time for them if their parents have time for each other. In contrast, children who seldom see their parents caring for or sharing with each other feel estrangement and distance. It is always true that a primary way to build and nourish warm relationships with our children is to build them with our spouse.

When our children were young, we set aside Friday for family night. Since there was no school the next day, no one had pressing homework to frustrate a leisurely, planned dinner hour. To make it more special, we didn't ask the children to change their clothes when they came home from school. We set the dining room table with a tablecloth, our best table service, and a favorite centerpiece. The menu included something everyone liked, and we ate dessert by candlelight.

Either we will take needed, loving time with our children when they are young, or they will demand angry, rebellious time when they grow older.

From the start of their marriage, spouses need to spend more time together for their own sake, for their children's sake, and for heaven's sake.

**For further thought:**
> *Would it be possible for you to write a covenant of time with your spouse which might include going out together alone once a week, and spending some time each day talking about what is happening and what you are feeling, and then praying together?*

# V.

# *Never Forget to Communicate*

# 1.

# A Commitment to Communicate

"We can't talk to each other."

"When we try to talk, we always end up arguing."

"I can't reach him."

"She doesn't understand me."

All married couples have, quite likely, thought or made statements like these. In ninety percent of all marital difficulties, communication is the major problem. The problems in the other ten percent are often directly or indirectly caused by the inability to communicate.

I believe this is true from my own experience of being married. Furthermore, through counseling many married couples, and from the conclusion of numerous scientific studies, I am persuaded that every marriage should begin with another covenant—the promise to communicate.

As Betty and I look back over our experience, we realize now that when we married, we assumed we would communicate. After all, we longed for times to talk and express our deepest feelings before we were married. While we dated, we schemed to do as many things together as possible. And we looked forward to marriage because then we could communicate without interruption as we learned to know each other more and more.

We assumed too much. We didn't make a definite commitment to communicate, and we became one of the statistics bearing out the study which shows most marriages experiencing a decreasing ability to communicate after the wedding vows. Why? Not because we planned it that way. In fact, we acknowledged that sometimes we failed to communicate because we didn't want to hurt the other, or we tried to ignore our feelings, thinking that our problems would go away.

Problems, however, do not disappear by our ignoring them. They only pile up, becoming inner irritations which build resentment and destroy love. Tiny trifles develop into tremendous vexations. Doubts grow in the shadows. Hiding our thoughts and feelings weakens the basic oneness of marital life. Only when we live in openness and honesty can we experience healing, help, and happiness. Only as we express our thoughts and feelings are "joys doubled and sorrows halved." Little things that we don't deal with multiply into unyielding giants which ruin relationships.

When children enter the family, communication patterns change. In fact, each spouse sees the other spending time with the children, so much so that a subtle jealously may creep in. Both may hesitate to mention their uneasiness, and gradually a breakdown of communication happens. This is a moment to stop and talk to each other.

At one such time for us, friends allowed us to use their cabin by the lake for a week. As we watched the children wade in the water and make sand castles, we were able to do some castle-building ourselves.

Meaningful marital communication starts when we share our deep inner feelings with each other honestly and openly. Then we are giving the best gift we can give—our real selves.

Moving to this deeper level of communication is difficult because it involves both risk and trust. How will my statements be taken? Will my spouse understand me? Will I be accepted after I bare my soul? Teenagers open themselves to their parents only to the point where they feel they are still loved and accepted. But that is true not only of teenagers. It is true of each of us. It requires trust to tell each other how we feel and what our needs are.

Lack of communication causes all kinds of misunderstandings. One day after we had been married for some years, I simply said to Betty without explanation, "Why don't you take care of the checkbook from now on?" Betty assumed responsibility for record-keeping at that point without my realizing that she did it with some resentment.

Several years later we were participating in a marriage seminar. I was explaining how often one marriage partner can do a job so much better than the other and, when we recognize that ability in the other, we can complement each other. To illustrate I said: "Betty is a much better bookkeeper than I am, so she keeps our checkbook. I was frustrated because the figures never came out right, and she keeps it in perfect shape."

To my surprise, Betty spoke up: "Now you tell me! I always resented that you told me to take care of the checkbook without any explanation. This finally clears the air." Numerous times Betty has referred to this as an example of how a short and clear explanation changed resentment into an understanding which makes the task enjoyable.

We often take each other's hand as we are ready to go to sleep at night. There have been a few times when we didn't feel friendly enough toward each other to follow this routine. For the most part, however, we cherish the practice as a final touch of love for the day.

Few, if any, joys exceed the wonder of a husband and wife who know how to share and care deeply, who freely express their feelings, ideals, and desires, knowing that, regardless what is expressed, each will continue to be loved and accepted.

**For further thought:**

> Why do you think many married partners experience a decreasing ability to communicate following their wedding vows?

# 2.

# *We Are Always Communicating*

Wallace Denton in *Family Problems and What to Do About Them* writes, "Ten years from now you may not remember much of this . . . but if you do recall anything, may it be this: the degree to which your marriage succeeds or fails will be closely related to your ability to communicate with each other, to understand and to be understood."

We are always communicating. Hundreds of bits of information are exchanged each minute between individuals communicating actively. Everything we do, every glance, tone of voice, even silence, is communication.

Although we usually center on the verbal, we realize that words are only a small part of communication. One expert suggests that we communicate only about seven percent by words. Perhaps about half our communication is body language—our facial expressions, touches, and gestures, which tell how we feel toward each other.

Much of our verbal communication is in our tone of voice. And much of the friction found in the average home comes from tone of voice. Long ago we learned that a child is much more aware of tone of voice than of specific words. A child is more alert to the way something is said than the instructions given.

But this is true not only of children. It is more true of all of us than we realize. And it is easy for marriage partners to develop a tone of voice which leads to distance rather than closeness.

Many times I have found in marriage counseling that we marry our opposites, so far as our ability or method of communicating. A young woman, for examples, marries a man who is more quiet than she. She enjoys his companionship because she loves to talk, and she has found someone who listens. He enjoys her because she is interesting, and, not being a great conversationalist, he needs and appreciates a person who makes up for this lack of his.

After the wedding vows, a pattern is likely to occur—unless it is headed off by some unusual personal insight. Frequently, a wife says, "He won't talk." Just as often, a husband complains, "She's always jabbering." The very communication patterns for which they chose and loved each other have become a source of irritation and battle. (This happens in other areas, as well!) She unrealistically expects that marriage will suddenly make him a different creature—one who now, in a few short months or years, becomes a flowing conversationalist. And he becomes annoyed by the very behavior that initially charmed him.

It is wise to realize that we are different personalities, and that there are many ways to communicate love—through touch, little gifts, silence in togetherness, a close caress, meaningfully looking into each other's eyes. Yet even so, poor or little communication is almost universally a problem in all unhappy marriages. Communication failure produces heartbreaking loneliness. Marriages flounder, not because of too much talking, but because of too little sharing of feelings and thinking.

Be alert—from the first day of your marriage—to those things that hinder communication. Early in a marriage a couple may communicate poorly out of good motives. Each worries about upsetting the other, and so both begin to hide their feelings and little hurts. Remember that love can handle all of this if it is in the open, far better than when it is hidden away.

Beware of the thieves of communication—not taking time together, getting involved in all kinds of side projects, watching TV, and a hundred other things, good in themselves, yet possible robbers of real communication.

Watch out for such destroyers of communication as sarcasm, ridicule, or making fun at the other's expense. Avoid the words, "You never" and "You always." These are barbs which hurt relationships and simply are not true. Steer clear of bringing up past failures. One man reporting on his wife said, "When I begin to talk, she becomes historical." "You mean *hysterical*," his friend said. "No, I mean *historical*. She brings up everything I ever did or said." Resurrecting past experiences as a rebuff or retort may result in cutting off necessary conversation.

Be careful of imagining that since you love each other and live so close to each other, you each must know how the other feels. This is not necessarily true. We are all highly individual in our past experiences, growth, perceptions, and reactions. We need to express how we feel if we want to be understood. It is also a mistake to say, "She/he doesn't know how I feel," if you have never explained exactly how you feel.

What is necessary for mature and loving communication? Listening is a critical piece of this mutual experience. To communicate is to try to hear the other's point of view, to understand what the other is feeling, and to empathize with each other. In order to communicate, a climate of trust, confidence, acceptance, and love is needed. We express only to the extent we are assured we will continue to be loved and accepted.

To communicate meaningfully in marriage, we must be willing to move to deeper levels of intimacy so that we can fully tell our fears, frustrations, and failures, as well as our joys, pleasures, and delights. True commitment is to drop pretense for self-disclosure and self-revelation.

A good marriage includes the commitment to communicate. It promises to avoid behavior which destroys openness, honesty, and freedom and instead practices acceptance, trust, and confidence.

### *For further thought:*

> *Do you agree or disagree with the statement that we share only to the extent we feel we will continue to be loved and accepted?*

# 3.

# *The Best Psychiatrists*

A man and a woman met one evening around the kitchen table. The couple had secured a divorce and now were together to decide how they would divide their furniture and other household items. Their discussion drifted to other subjects and concerns. After several hours of talking the man said, "Why in the world couldn't we talk like this before?"

What brings alienation, separation, and divorce? Shortage of money? Sexual incompatibility? Temperamental differences? Clashing over such matters, and many other areas like these, are only symptoms of an overall problem. The number one family problem is a problem of communication.

Inability to communicate effectively shows up, to some degree, in eighty-five out of one hundred couples visiting marriage counselors. Many times it is their only problem. Most times it lies at the basis of their other problems. Scores of others who do not know how to communicate meaningfully go directly to the divorce courts without seeking help.

Though lack of communication is the most common problem in marriage, and no marriage is entirely free of communication difficulties, it is one of the easiest to deal with if persons really want to have a successful relationship.

We can learn to communicate because we have the God-given ability to do so—and because each of us has the deep desire to do so. "Communicate" means, in fact, to share one's soul with another. We want to express our deepest hopes, fears, and joys—and have them be heard and understood. One of our deepest desires is to give and receive love without reservation.

Husbands and wives ought to be each other's best therapists. Why? Because, first, love is present and, second, because many psychological needs are best met by simply telling someone our feelings and emotions.

By communicating our thoughts and fears we release tension and unburden our minds. We need each other as sounding boards to clarify our feelings, thoughts, ideas, and plans. Open communication can lift us out of loneliness, dissolve our feelings of isolation, and make our worries seem far less important. And who should be better able to do this than our spouses?

Regardless of our current communication patterns as husband and wife, ten years from now they can and will be even better than we imagine, if we are willing to learn to communicate. Without constant and clear communication, the greatest lovers and the best marriages in the world sink into mediocrity or disastrous divorce. Without communication, misunderstandings develop, resentments smolder, and lovers drift apart.

While we were dating, we learned to know each other by communicating. During those days we set aside time to be together. We went places. We found more and more things to do and talk about. Much of our communication was non-verbal—looking into each other's eyes, holding each other's hand, giving little gifts, and exchanging loving glances. Finally, through all this communicating, we learned to know each other well enough that we agreed to get married and to spend the rest of life learning to know each other better.

In a short time, what two people longed for most can be lost if meaningful communication stops. Good marriages do not miraculously materialize out of passion and principles of family loyalty. They grow because of commitment, compassion, and communication skills.

If a husband and wife are to avoid the disappointments of many marriages, they will need to covenant together to take time and effort to courageously communicate honestly. They will, in a loving and caring way, express all that needs to be shared to keep their marriage growing in communication.

**For further thought:**

*Give examples of your best ways of communicating with each other.*

# 4.
# Communication—A Real Test

"What is a monologue, Daddy?" Alex wanted to know. "It is a conversation between a husband and wife, son," his father replied. "But," said Alex, "our teacher said that's a dialogue." "Your teacher isn't married," his father answered.

All the jokes about marriage are about people who live in the dip, who have an impaired ability to talk together or to understand each other.

In business, ignoring good communication means inefficiency, loss of profit, and failure. In international affairs, lack of communication or wrong communication builds mistrust and suspicion and leads to war.

In marriage, poor communication means frustration, fear, unhappiness, resentment, rebellion, and disillusionment, and leads to divorce. The level at which we communicate is the level at which we live. Family breakdown invariably begins with some form of failure in communication.

Unless we understand each other, we cannot meet each other's needs. So we must constantly strive to share our feelings, our thoughts, our desires—all that is important to us.

We communicate by all we say and do. We disclose ourselves through our attitudes, gestures, and silences. We use the hidden meanings in the words we say and in our very responses to life itself. We are always expressing something. A wife who says, "I can't communicate with my husband. He doesn't talk," needs to understand that her husband is communicating by his silence.

One woman said to her friend, "Did you ever hear of the great stone face?" "Yes, I think I have," her friend replied. "I married him," the first responded. The question is why the husband has become silent.

We learned to know each other by communicating. So why do we become silent? Simply entering the intimacy of marriage does not guarantee that good communication will happen. It is possible to live together for a long time, and even to talk a lot, without really understanding or knowing each other.

Often when counseling a couple who has been married for many years, I have heard one spouse respond in this way to a comment by his or her marriage partner: "I never knew you felt that way," or "I told you a million times." Somehow we don't get through. We have ways of blocking each other out.

When there is meaningful communication in marriage, it is the result of a continuous, conscious, and concerted effort on the part of both partners to get through to each other. It doesn't just happen.

Nonverbal communication can be positive or negative. A loving pat can say "I love you," as well as words. A loving look, a tender touch, a small gift chosen with care can say a great deal.

Bonaro W. Overstreet in her article "Growing Together or Apart" says, "For some men, romantic words of love seem too soft for married manhood. Wise is the wife who contents herself with a husband's sharing of business problems, his asking her to go with him to a meeting or just for a walk, his warm look across the table in the midst of the children's chatter, or the patient hours he spends weeding the garden or shoveling snow."

On the other hand, verbal communication will always be important. Talking is one of the tests of true love. Listening is also one of the tests of caring love—especially listening with the third ear.

With our third ear we hear what persons mean behind the words they say. When a wife says to her husband, "I had an especially busy day. What do you want for supper?", she may be asking to go out to eat. It is important that he respond to the hidden message.

When we discuss communicating, we are not talking just about what will add to marriage or improve it. We are speaking of the very breath of marriage. Communication must be practiced or a marriage will deteriorate. The more partners can discuss and sense each other's feelings, the closer they become as husband and wife.

If a married couple takes time each day to share their feelings in meaningful conversation, they will probably find that the problems between them simply dissolve and disappear. They are able to develop a deep bond which transcends the petty disturbances standing in the way of a happy, growing marriage.

### For further thought:

*Why is it important to listen with your "third ear"? What negatives might you encounter in reading something into what another says?*

# 5.
# The "What" Level of Communication

In Charles Shultz's comic strip, Lucy shouts at Linus, "You Blockhead!" and Linus counters, "What did you call me . . . a dumbbell?" Lucy replies, "I didn't say 'dumbbell'; I said 'blockhead!'" Reflecting with her chin in her hands, her elbows resting on the top of the wall, Lucy says to herself, "That's what causes so much trouble between people today . . . there is no real understanding."

Our aim in marriage must be to move to deeper levels of communication and understanding, to move from the mediocre to the meaningful. Not only is it essential to give each other certain information and to be able to tell our partners what we think about issues, we must move deeper and express how we feel. We must move beyond the "what" to the "who" level in communication.

How do I describe "what" communication? Take a couple of typical "what" level communicators, Phil and Jane, who came to a marriage enrichment retreat. I was glad since it's usually impossible to get this kind of couple anywhere near a discussion about communication or marriage. They believe they can't communicate. They usually assume there is no hope for them. They worry that they may be asked to talk to each other in the presence of the whole group.

Phil and Jane operate on the instructional level of "what" communication. They live together. But they talk together only about those things which must be done around the house. So when Phil comes home from work, Jane reports things like the following: "Phil, the electric bill is due." "Sarah misbehaved at school again today." "I'll need money for groceries if I'm to get them." "The children must have new clothes before school starts."

What does Phil communicate? He says things like: "Before you use the car tomorrow you ought to stop for gas." "If we're to make that noon appointment, you'd better have the children ready by eleven." "I'll be home late on Friday."

All Phil and Jane do is communicate instructions. They reveal nothing about themselves, how they feel, what they are thinking inside. They say only what they need to in order to get along. The information they share consists of facts or instructions, necessary for the family to function.

Another level of "what" communication is informational. Jim and Barb illustrate this level well. They also came to a marriage enrichment retreat. They are quite sociable. They may even consider themselves good communicators and persons of great openness. As Barb expresses it, "We thought we were good at talking together. We talked about a lot of things—books we read, places we traveled, our day's work, what we heard, the preacher's sermon, as well as all kinds of ideas we encountered."

Jim thought the same. He said to the group, "Barb and I have always felt free to talk. We meet with a small group and have lots of friends who visit. We never lack for things to say at our house."

But at the retreat, as the discussion moved to the feeling level and into areas of personal struggle and differences, Jim and Barb seemed to have a new world opened to them. When some began to talk about inner conflicts and reveal how they experienced themselves and their relationship,

Jim and Barb felt left out. When they did begin to articulate their feelings, they found themselves saying, "I never knew you felt like that." "You never told me that bothered you." "I had no idea that was a problem for you." Jim and Barb were surprised at how little they really knew about each other's fears, feelings, desires, aspirations, and expectations.

Jim and Barb are the kind of couple who are able to discuss all sorts of ideas and concerns outside themselves, often in eloquent and intriguing ways, yet without revealing anything about their personal selves. They seldom share their souls with each other. They have friends with whom they can chat about many topics, but they seldom reveal to their friends or to each other their deep inner feelings and the struggles they have.

Such communication fosters only surface relationships. Although they talk much, these people's conversations remain on the informational level. They offer what they know, based on what they have heard, read, or seen, but they express little about themselves and who they really are inside.

Most of this "informational" communication is simply a playback of what we have absorbed or is a reflection of what we think about events or other persons. It moves one step beyond the instructional level to include telling what we think. But this kind of communication still remains superficial and has little meaning because it does not reveal who we are and what is happening inside us—what makes us sad or glad.

"What" communicators tell only "what" they think or hear—not "who" they are or how they feel. "Do you think," a woman asked at a recent retreat, "that many people live at the 'what' level?" "Unfortunately, yes," I answered. Those who study human nature explain that love can only grow as we reveal ourselves more fully. That fact means, therefore, that many persons do not experience a growing love relationship, the kind that God intends and the kind which brings the continual excitement of new discovery.

**For further thought:**
> *Although the "what" level is necessary if we are to live and work together, do you believe it is possible to grow together at this level?*

# 6.
# The "Who" Level
# of Communication

To communicate who we are is to reveal or to share our personhood with another. It is to express that which is completely me, which is different from any other.

It means more than to merely voice surface feelings, such as whether I feel good or bad, happy or sad. These feelings are usually easy to detect in the intimacy of friendship and marriage without much effort.

To come to the "who" level of communication is to arrive at the place where I begin to tell my marriage partner my deep inner feelings of fear, frustration, hate, hurt, anger, love, joy, satisfaction, and pride, the temptations and aspirations which are really and truly mine.

In marriage, God intends us to become "one flesh" which includes, but is more than, sexual union. It is the uncovering of ourselves before each other to reveal "who" we are. We strip away our roles and take off our masks and protective armor and stand stark naked before each other to reveal our inner selves.

At this level of communication we begin a great adventure—that of real growth together. We begin to understand not only what we do but why we do the things we do. Marriage presents the greatest potential for humans to grow in a relationship, but only if we learn to communicate at this "who" level of inner feelings, sharing ourselves fully with one another.

Eric Fromm in *The Art of Loving* wrote,"Love is possible only if two persons communicate with each other from the center of their existence . . . "

I found among my wife's notes this helpful statement: "To love God is to let God love me. To let God love me is to let God know me. To let God know me is to be open to help. To be open to God results in the unbelievable experience of daring to love myself. I am loved by God!"

Applying this to the marriage relationship we might say, "To love my marriage partner is to let my partner really know me. And to let my partner know me is to be completely open. This results in the unbelievable experience of knowing myself and daring to love myself." As I am discovered, I sense a release, and I desire more and more the enlivening experience of fuller revelation. And I sense more and more my own potential for unity and for belonging to my partner.

A couple approaching marriage actually knows very little of each other. But what they know they like, and they know they want to know each other better.

Paul Tournier in *To Understand Each Other* said, "In such an adventure, each partner in marriage develops. Each is able to go beyond the natural reflexes of his personality type and his own sex. There is a complete exchange. Each gives the other that precious dimension of his personality, and each gives the other that which is most missing. It is no longer a question of masculine or feminine love, but of a much deeper love in which each particular aspect of love is not realized until they are sure that they no longer have anything hidden from each other."

Communication involves knowing and understanding the deeper levels of each other's personality, and being willing to share in such a way that each can safely and without embarrassment expose herself or himself emotionally to the other. Fear of rejection, condemnation, or estrangement causes persons to wear masks and keep their feelings to themselves, often locked away for good.

When we marry, we come together with mixed feelings. We come together in love, which means, among other things, that we know and care for the other the way she or he is, and we want to learn to know each other more fully.

We also come into marriage with some concern that our spouse might not love us if we reveal all our inner feelings and fears. We want to be known, yet we fear being known too well lest we be rejected, lest we become unacceptable, or lest we lose the trust of the other.

Yet it is when we are loved, when we are part of the intimacy of marriage, that we should be able to move safely beyond the "what" level to the "who" level of communicating. We should be able to come to the most complete understanding of ourselves—our problems and possibilities. The "who" level has unending opportunities for a husband and wife to grow together in every aspect of life. It is the unending hope of marriage.

**For further thought:**
> *What has helped you move to the deeper levels of "who" communication?*

# 7.
# Why the "Who" Level Is So Difficult

Few, if any of us, are prepared for the "who" level of communicating. Many parents don't allow their children the time to talk in an open, accepting atmosphere about the inner happenings of their hearts and minds. Few parents make the effort, or even know how, to talk about feelings, inner thoughts, and why we respond the way we do.

Children are told that they should not be angry, should not cry, should not feel toward others the way they do. And so they learn to stifle and bury within the inner cries and emotions of childhood. We grow to adulthood with our feelings bottled up, fearful of sharing who we really are.

Throughout life we are identified by our jobs, our degrees, our material possessions, whose children we are, and who our spouse is. All these identification marks tell only what we do and have—not who we are.

We are not prepared for "who" communicting in our educational system. The great Greek teacher Socrates long ago gave a clue to heading off personal problems by telling his pupils that it was of first importance to "Know thyself." Yet school instruction still centers around "what." A person can easily move from kindergarten through graduate school, gaining almost no self-understanding while getting an abundance of knowledge and information by instruction.

Because we emphasize knowing facts instead of ourselves, many teachers have little understanding of themselves or of their students. This leads to all kinds of ridiculous requirements, responses, and reactions by teachers and pupils. A highly regimented school system, geared to the mass communication of facts, has little place for enabling students to develop in self-understanding. The structure is given to knowing "what" instead of "why."

Often our religious lives are not open to personal sharing and self-understanding. The heart of many people's religion is made up of "do's" and "don'ts" rather than "being." "Being" ought to be the heart of religion. Instead, we are told not to feel a certain way, not to react in a certain manner, or not to do certain things, rather than being helped to self-understanding. Religion too often tells us what not to do, think, or feel. It fails to help us see why we are as we are; it neglects to show us how to use the resources of religion to become what God intends.

A serious reading of the Bible gives a person much self-understanding. The Bible holds tremendous psychological and sociological insights and understandings. Yet much religious teaching and preaching involves pounding in more and more facts, taboos, and warnings, rather than disclosing and grasping who God says we are—persons of worth filled with God-given feelings and capabilities. One of the major reasons we as husbands and wives need to work so deliberately to achieve real communication, revealing to each other who we actually are, is that from birth on, many influences work against this kind and depth of communication.

A wife in her early thirties came for counsel. She was deeply discouraged. She was sure that it was no use trying to start all over again. She said, "I feel so numb and hurt that I don't know if I want to try making our marriage a success." She told me that their communication was dead. As a counselor I gave her the guidance and encouragement I could.

The next day her husband called and said he wanted to talk. He shared his deep disappointment. "Oh, yes," he said, toward the end of the session, "my wife said, 'Make sure you ask him how we start again.'" Then I sensed hope.

**For further thought:**
What reasons do you think make the "who" level of communication difficult?

# 8.
# *Some Communication Essentials*

Paul Tournier in *To Understand Each Other* tells about his acquaintance with an American colleague, a surgeon from New York. They liked each other but had difficulty understanding one another because Tournier knew few English words and the surgeon knew few French words. Yet they managed to get through to each other, because both ardently wanted to communicate.

There is no question that better communication skills would improve how we listen to our children, could change our educational system, and might even correct our religious approach. A few basic suggestions may help a husband and wife begin to communicate more satisfyingly.

Each must be sincerely open to understanding. Tournier observes that when you listen to the conversation of many couples, it sounds "for the most part [like] dialogues of the deaf. Each one speaks primarily in order to set forth his own ideas, words to justify himself, in order to enhance himself and to accuse others. Exceedingly few exchanges of viewpoints manifest a real desire to understand the other person."

First, each of us needs to decide if we really want to communicate at the deeper "who" level. Because of past experiences or personal inhibitions, we may believe that it is simply impossible to share the inner recesses of our souls—

our weaknesses and mistakes as well as our ambitions and our views. We need to mutually agree (although one partner may need to take the lead) and determine together to move from the "what" to the "who" level in communicating. We will need to be vulnerable and, at times, to pay some price for that vulnerability.

It is difficult to bare myself, especially my faults, to the very person whose love I long for and whose respect I want more than anything else. But courageously confessing and expressing my deepest self frequently calls forth a reciprocal confession and sharing from my partner. That is a wonderfully joyful experience, akin to sensing the grace of God who accepts and loves us as we are. We can begin by *sharing* ourselves rather than blaming each other. Why not try to understand each other, and understand why our spouse feels the way she or he does?

Second, we need to begin slowly, a little at a time, using moments when we feel especially close and loving. Timing can be of supreme importance. Melodie Davis writes, "The bubble first burst the day after our wedding on the eight-hour car trip to our honeymoon spot. I crushed my husband with the words, 'I'd better warn you; I like to have time to myself. I don't know how it'll be—living with another person twenty-four hours a day.'

"That wasn't exactly a new revelation to my husband, Stuart, but he didn't think these were very encouraging words with which to begin a honeymoon. 'Bad timing' we termed it later when we could laugh about it. I was so eager to have an honest, open relationship in which we'd tell each other exactly how we were feeling that I'd forgotten the incredibly important element of timing."

Although sometimes it is helpful to blurt out my negative feelings, I need to be sure my spouse can take it. A pastor friend of mine said he could not fully express his feelings of love to his wife until he was able to articulate his anger. His wife was strong and loving enough to absorb his anger and then receive his fuller love. The more we reveal ourselves to each other, the more we are aware of when and what to share.

This kind of in-depth give-and-take needs to be done with much discretion. To be healing, it must happen from a desire to help rather than to hurt. Love, of course, is basic to such involvement and communicating.

We need to remember that feelings themselves are not wrong. Feelings have no morality. We may think that we should not feel a certain way. But the fact is that we *do* feel that way. It is best to accept our feelings and to state them. Then we are prepared to ask why we feel the way we do and deal with that question.

Third, we must keep making the effort. Communication is not something we do once and for all, or one hour a week, or in several sessions a year. We must try to take some time each day to discuss our feelings, aspirations, and inner struggles with each other. The more we unveil our inner selves in the love relationship of marriage, the more we will experience healing and purifying. Living together in this way will not solve all our problems, but it can be the start of many solutions, and it will certainly further meaningful communication.

Once we have experienced mutual sharing and understanding, we will simply want more. Nothing helps me to open up quite as much as sensing that my life partner wants to understand me.

As we share at the "who" level on a regular basis, we develop a deep bond of oneness and experience a new richness, growth, and understanding. As soon as we begin to hide matters from each other, we compromise that openness and oneness so essential to having a satisfying marriage. We begin a pattern of marital frustration, fear, and failure.

The Bible for many centuries has reminded people, "Confess your faults one to another and pray one for another that you may be healed" (James 5:19). We are beginning to understand a little of what that means.

### *For further thought:*

> *Review the essentials for open communication and list additional ideas you have found helpful.*

# 9.
# Our Different Love Languages

Gary Chapman, a marriage and family counselor in Winston-Salem, North Carolina, describes five main love languages.* He tells us that, although we each need all five expressions of love, each of us has a primary love language. It is the one which makes us feel especially loved.

Most of us express love the way we feel the need to be loved, rather than the way our spouse may feel the need to be loved. Many husbands and wives have different love languages. And so we go on, trying to get through to our spouse, wondering why our spouse doesn't respond as we wish, never realizing that our love languages are different.

The first love language which Chapman discusses is love through words. That seems natural enough. But the fact is that only a small percentage of our total communication is verbal. Body language and tone of voice are of great significance.

Words are the primary love language for many of us. When someone says, "I love you," "You are the best cook," or "You are the best provider," the recipient feels deeply loved. Words are likely to be this person's primary love language.

A second language is giving gifts. Gifts say he or she loves me, cares about me, thought enough about me to take time (and maybe even was inconvenienced), in order to express love for me. The recipient is filled with love and feels especially cared for when receiving a gift. The size of the gift is not important. Charles Shedd says it can be a rose in a gargle bottle. But a card, a letter, a gift says, "I am loved."

Third, Gary says action is a primary love language. The person whose primary love language is action is inclined to reason, "You say you love me, but I would like to see you do something. If you would help me with the dishes, make me a special meal, clean up the place, I'd know you love me."

I remember one couple in their late forties who came to my office for help in their marriage. In our conversation the husband said, "She wants me to express love. I'd like her to clean up the place." The wife replied, "He never appreciates it anyway." He said, "It's been a long time since she made a decent meal." She commented, "He never says 'thank you' if I do." The husband wanted action to feel loved. She wanted a small expression of appreciation and love.

At another time a woman came to talk to me about an article I had written. In it I suggested that as long as there is one thing you can do to build love, it will be worth it all. She told me that she had spent a good part of a day making a very special meal for her husband. He came home and ate the meal without a word of appreciation. The next day a dozen roses were delivered to her door. She said, "I was so furious that I refused to receive them."

What had happened? She wanted only a few words of love. Her husband tried to express his love with a gift of roses. They missed each other.

Time is the fourth love language. For the person whose primary language is time, this means undivided attention. It is not simply sitting in the same room watching the same TV program. Instead, it is taking time to look into each other's eyes, to do something together beyond the routine, to go for a walk, to hold each other close.

Time is a big issue. It generates the great complaint of

wives in particular. If couples spent as little time being truly together before they were married as many do after they become husband and wife, many marriages would never happen.

Touch is the fifth primary love language. Touch has always been a way of communicating love—a caress, a loving kiss, and a tender hug.

Gary Chapman, in discussing these, emphasizes that we need to express our love for each other, not only in the way we like to be loved, but also in the way our partner feels loved. Try it! It is good advice for showing love to our spouse, our children, and beyond.

**For further thought:**
> *What is your primary love language? Your spouse's? How have you tried to express your love?*

---

\* *I am indebted to Gary Chapman and his article, "How Do I Say I Love You," published in* Christian Herald, *June 1987, pages 21, 22, 24. The five love languages are Chapman's; the expansion of those ideas are mine.*

# 10.
## Conflict Is Normal

David and Vera Mace offer interesting and encouraging insight into marital conflict. "We began by seeing conflict as something bad and avoiding it. Then we shifted to the view that we had to endure it with fortitude. It came as a revelation to us to learn that conflicts in marriage are really 'growth points' to be used as opportunities to deepen our understanding of ourselves and of each other, and to change for the better.

"What made a drastic difference to us was when we came to understand the positive function of anger in a close relationship. We had begun with the conventional view that anger is sinful, or at least an undesirable emotion. When we found that anger is in fact the defense system of the inner self, that only love and anger working harmoniously together can keep a marriage in healthy balance—that was a vital turning point in our relationship."

Every vital marriage has conflicts. What we need to realize is that conflict can be the beginning of something creative, producing growth and new depth of love.

Evelyn Millis Duvall in a Public Affairs Pamphlet, *Building Your Marriage,* gives good guidance about how to quarrel constructively. "If you must quarrel, there is a knack to it that every married person should learn. Certain techniques are downright harmful. Others are rather risky. Some are almost universally constructive. You quarrel constructively when you finish with your marriage stronger than when you began. Here are some ways in which it can be done.

"1. Accept the fact of the conflict without shame or pretending it isn't there. Remember that conflict is normal. Face the fact that you and your spouse are human beings. Don't be alarmed when differences arise from time to time.

"2. Try to find out what the whole thing means to your mate. What's 'eating' him or her? How does he/she feel about it and why? Keep as calm as you can yourself while you encourage him/her to talk it all out.

"3. What does it matter to you? Ask yourself honestly why it is that you are so excited about it? (For instance, Andrew discovered that he got riled whenever his wife set her mouth in a thin, little line because that habit was associated in his experience with an extremely dominating aunt who made his life miserable when he was a little boy.)

"4. Adopt a problem-solving approach to the situation, but keep remembering that many situations need not really become problems. On the basis of your mutual acceptance and understanding, try to see what can be done to work things out comfortably. Don't let tensions pile up day after day. Work them out as they come along.

"5. Try to agree on some next step for taking care of the situation. Get busy on it together as soon as possible.

"6. Do what you can to help the other to save face, to feel stronger, to feel your love, no matter what. Avoid sniping at each other. Keep your energy focused on the *problem* as much as you can—rather than on the *other's fault.*

"7. Be patient. Be willing to take a little time for the solving of your difficulties. Don't expect miracles. Count on spending some time on the problem.

"8. When the whole situation gets beyond you, get some competent counseling help."

(Public Affairs Pamphlet No. 113, 381 Park Avenue South, New York, New York, pp. 23-24.)

**For further thought:**

>   How have you viewed conflict?—As a bad thing to avoid at any cost? Or as a creative thing which produces growth?

# VI.

# Magnify Assets— Minimize Liabilities

# 1.
# *Accent the Positive*

A woman threw down a "Dear Abby" column on my desk. "There, read that!" she said. "It's my husband exactly." I read the column. It was written by a woman who described her husband, among other things, as a workaholic who didn't have time for his wife, a man who did not express his love in words and who was not, in general, a loving and tender person.

"You say this sounds like your husband?" I asked.

"Exactly," she replied.

"Since your husband isn't here for me to talk with," I went on, "let me ask you several questions. First of all, is your husband faithful to you?"

"Oh yes," she said. "I have no reason to doubt his faithfulness."

"And how does he relate to the children?" I asked.

"Oh, the kids like him. Yes, he relates rather well to the children."

"One more question. Does he provide well for you?"

"That's a big part of the problem," she reflected. "He works all the time."

We talked for a while about her husband, and then I ventured, "Without excusing your husband in any way, I must tell you that many wives would be happy for a faithful and industrious husband who has a good relationship with his children. You have a lot to build on and appreciate."

We discussed for some time how she might relate to her

husband so as to draw him into a more loving and tender relationship, and how she might initiate planning special times together. As she left my study that day, she paused at the door, "Am I ever glad you told me what's good about my husband!"

Soon after getting married, partners may find themselves zeroing in on the negative in their spouse, rather than focusing on what is good. And each of us does have a negative side.

In the wedding vows, both persons covenant "to bear with each other's infirmities and weaknesses." One of the most memorable questions asked of those who marry is, "Do you take the person by your side for better and for worse?" The wedding vows are quite realistic.

We found out soon after our wedding what we may not have fully faced up to before—that each of us had (and still has) strengths and weaknesses. Each has a better and a worse side. And the "worse side" can be terribly unromantic, irritating, and sometimes downright unbearable.

As so often happens, we were each attracted to our opposite. The rather shy person was drawn to the one who, because of a good sense of humor, is often the life of the party, one who feels comfortable in any situation. It was appealing to be able to join in the laughter and good times. It was a pleasure to be with friends and then rehearse the fun-filled evening together.

We were surprised to discover that marriage switched the dynamics all around. The outgoing one became irritated when the other was quiet and had little to say. Only when we each recognized that we were being irritated by what was really a strength in the other person, could we constructively deal with our differences.

In order to be happy, we have needed to pledge to magnify the good qualities for which we chose each other and to minimize the "worse" traits which tag along. This does not mean that we refuse to help each other overcome undesirable traits. It does mean, however, that we resist allowing these characteristics from becoming the center of attention and concern. After all, none of us changes until we feel loved and accepted as we are.

When we magnify each other's assets, we begin to see that our spouse, in spite of faults, is better than we imagined and possesses qualities we need and appreciate deeply.

In his *Letters to Malcolm*, C.S. Lewis wrote, "Nothing which is at all times and in every way agreeable to us can have objective reality. It is the very nature of the real that it should have sharp corners and rough edges, that it should be resistant, should be itself. Dream furniture is the only kind on which you never stub your toes or bang your knee. You and I have both known happy marriages. But how different wives were from the imaging mistress of our adolescent dreams. So much less exquisitely adopted to our wishes; and for that reason (among others) so incomparably better."

### For further thought:

How can you purposefully center on the positive traits of your spouse? In premarital counseling I ask each person to bring a list of ten things which each deeply appreciates in the other person. We talk about them. Then I say, "Now frame them. Put them in some prominent place. After marriage we easily forget the good."

Why not make a list of ten things you appreciate about your spouse?

# 2.
# We Are Different Persons

One professional counselor described her own experience: "At the lowest point in our marriage I went back to my journal which I kept during my dating years. I found that all the wonderful things I had written about Gary were still true. Yet I had been letting myself dwell on the negatives I saw. And it pulled our marriage to its lowest point." She observed that when she began to focus on these good traits, the marriage changed for the better.

We need to recognize that some "worse" traits will probably never change a great deal. For example, a talkative person may choose to marry a more silent type. After marriage the talkative one might try to turn the silent one into an outgoing conversationalist. Such a person will probably never become talkative. Forget it!

Many of us marry persons for the traits we ourselves do not have. Once we're married, our job is to learn to appreciate the traits, temperament, and characteristics the other has. If we do, we will see that these qualities help to make us well-rounded persons.

Each partner has gifts and assets to contribute to the marriage, and the more these are recognized and respected, the happier the marriage. To marry an equal does not mean that one of us cannot do things better than the other. A marriage is strengthened by receiving and encouraging the abilities of two people. Studies show that in strong marriages spouses have learned to maximize each other's gifts. The more areas in which I feel respect and reception, the more satisfying is my marriage.

It is best, we have learned, not to compare our marriage with others. Each person comes from a different background. Each person has different views and expectations. "The goal of marriage," says Richard Dobbs, "is not to think alike, but to think together." Being different does not mean that one is better or worse than the other.

In one marriage the wife takes care of servicing and cleaning the car and mowing the lawn. The husband takes care of the checkbook. This works well because of the interests and abilities of each. The opposite may be true in another marriage. We are happiest when we enable each other to do what each enjoys and is most capable of doing. To compare one marriage with another, or to think that there are preferred patterns, is to ruin relationships and to ignore abilities.

While we may recognize our special and separate gifts before and immediately after marriage, we may discover other gifts and abilities only after some time together. It took us a number of years to realize that one of us was a much better accountant. The other enjoyed gardening and assumed responsibility there. In many other ways we can appreciate, enjoy, and profit from the differing gifts and interests of each other.

We must also learn to appreciate each other's differences in personality and perceptions. For a husband and wife to look at issues from different points of view can be a great help because it gives a broader perspective. When spouses are able to understand this, two partners can build each other up rather than do battle.

Marriage is a complementary relationship. Complementary suggests the blending of two distinct entities to make both better. As we accept and appreciate what the other is, we become greater persons than we could ever be alone.

**For further thought:**

*In what ways do you see yourselves complementing each other?*

# 3.
# We Can Learn to Affirm

Too often we are like the old Vermont farmer who sat on his porch whittling, his wife beside him rocking and knitting. After a long, long silence the old man said, "You know, Sarah, you have meant so much to me that sometimes it's more'n I can stand not to tell you about it!" Affirmation and praise cause love to flourish, just as water refreshes a flower.

Affirmation is a basic cohesive factor in all happy marriage relationships. We have learned that the impulse to criticize usually grows out of our own inadequacy, guilt, or jealousy. The ability to compliment, to appreciate, to accept, and to see the good in another reveals a secure person with inner peace, self-acceptance, and understanding. This is someone who can admit failure and mistakes.

Few of us respond positively to negative criticism. Criticism may change our actions, but it is of no help in altering our attitudes, which are far more basic. We are all inclined to become more caring, thoughtful, and generous, and the person we long to be, when someone notices and encourages our good qualities.

So when we encourage and appreciate our spouse, we are not only helping that person be better, we are also increasing our own self-worth and strengthening the relationship on which our marital happiness hinges.

The same is also true in relation to our children. The child who is constantly criticized becomes critical. But, of even greater consequence, the child becomes unsure, insecure, attacking others in many ways, and developing little self-esteem.

When as parents we magnify the assets and minimize the liabilities of our child, the child develops self-confidence and learns the qualities of graciousness and acceptance, so basic to all of life. The kind of behavior husband and wife practice between themselves usually extends to the way they treat their children.

Some time ago we participated in a delightful wedding. Near the close of the ceremony, the bride and groom asked those attending for advice about being married. "Some of you have been married a long time," they said. "You have learned what is important for a successful and happy marriage. We are starting. What advice do you have for us?"

Among the numerous significant suggestions was one given by a grandmother. "I believe your marriage will be happy," she said, "if each day you express one thing you appreciate about the other."

**For further thought:**
> *For what qualities or practices do you feel most affirmed?*

# 4.
# *Humor Helps*

Norman Cousins, the well-known editor, philosopher, and speaker, developed serious pain in his joints. His doctors agreed that he had a life-threatening disease for which they had few answers.

Cousins checked himself out of the hospital and into the cheerful environment of a hotel. He had read about the role that negative emotions play on the chemical balance of the body. By watching funny movies and old "Candid Camera" segments, and by following certain dietary regimens, Norman Cousins began the road to recovery.

Cousins found that one ten-minute period of laughter gave him two hours of painless sleep. Ten years later, he was back to his maximum level, having reversed all previous medical predictions.

Many marriages could also experience release from a lot of pain and find new life if the persons involved exercised a little humor. Married couples are inclined to take themselves too seriously. It is a cherished gift to be able to laugh at myself. Students of human nature point out that humor releases stress, resolves conflict, motivates, and energizes, thereby inducing a creative, problem-solving state of mind. Humor gains attention and gives our communication greater impact. Humor helps us adjust to the imponderables in life and helps us survive until conditions change and problems can be solved. Humor helps to relieve and to prevent negative emotional stress.

Victor Borge, the Danish-born pianist said, "Laughter is the shortest distance between two people." As the 19th-century English novelist William Makepeace Thackeray wrote, "A good laugh is sunshine in the house." Dr. Harvey Mindness, an Antioch University psychologist, noted in his book *Laughter and Liberation,* "Humor expands awareness and broadens perspective."

A kind of expanded awareness was displayed by a recent national Teacher of the Year. On her eighteenth wedding anniversary she sent herself one red rose accompanied by the message, "I love you," and the signature, "Jim," on the card. Her husband Jim was startled to learn when he received a bill from the florist that he had remembered their anniversary.

Many times we take ourselves so seriously that we cut lines of communication. One husband, after a year or two of marriage, asked, "Where is the happy woman I married?" Why does a spouse become a grumpy old grouch after marriage? One factor may be taking oneself too seriously.

As one psychologist wrote, "The lack of ability to find humor in life is a sign of poor mental health."

Every marriage will have its tedious, trying, tense times. Such experiences can provide opportunity to demonstrate that our happiness does not depend upon circumstances, but flows from deep within. Of all persons, Christians ought to demonstrate this reality.

A friend told me this story. "Early in our marriage we had pie for supper. It was Mary's first try at making a pie crust. Some days after she served the pie, she found out that I had, on the sly, slipped the crust to the dog. Mary was pretty upset. When I got home, she told me so in no uncertain terms. I was quiet for a little bit, and then I said, 'Mary, I was afraid for a while that even the dog wouldn't eat it.'

With that we both burst into laughter and fell into each other's arms."

"At that moment," said Mary, "Don and I pledged to discuss everything together. We promised to be open and frank with each other and not hide our thoughts and feelings again. Believe it or not, we are still friends after fifteen years."

Love has a sense of humor. We are not fun to live with if we take ourselves too seriously. We will be hurt at every turn. Love gives us room to laugh as long as we are not belittling another, and as long as we are laughing with and not at another. Laughing and being humorous dare never happen at another's expense. A joke can be a put-down, a subtle attack on a spouse, or a cruel attempt to change or criticize. This kind of humor can only hurt, damage relationships, and leave scars.

We can learn a valuable lesson from the comedian Bob Hope. For more than fifty years Hope has told jokes on himself rather than on the other person. No wonder people love him!

I believe we can develop, by God's and each other's help, a joyful spirit. That is a fruit of the Spirit. One of the clearest statements on the role of humor and health and happiness is in Proverbs 17:22: "A cheerful heart is a good medicine, but a downcast spirit dries up the bones."

**For further thought:**
*Has your ability to laugh diminished or grown during your marriage?*

# 5.

# *What Makes My Husband Easy to Live With*

In a series of marriage retreats and seminars, wives were asked what particular trait or characteristic made their husbands easy to live with. Here is a sampling of typical replies that husbands may want to consider in the interest of promoting happier relationships. This is what wives appreciate about their husbands. Names are changed, of course.

*Martin and Meals.* "During our six years of marriage, Martin has let me know he appreciates my cooking. He never compares me with his mother who is a great cook! Beyond his regular compliments about my cooking, he often gives me a heartfelt kiss, which makes me feel that my efforts are worthwhile."

*Frank's Fun to Live With.* "My husband, Frank, is simply exciting to live with. There's never a dull moment when he's around. He's happy and gives people a good laugh. This spirit also makes him a good father to our kids."

*Fairness Is Foremost.* "One of my husband's most prominent qualities that makes him easy to live with is his fairness. It's a characteristic I hadn't noticed before we were married, but now that I live with him, I see it clearly. He's willing to take his share of responsibility around the house and with our children. He is not a particularly affectionate man, but because he shares so willingly, his love comes shining through."

*Lester Listens.* "I can tell my husband loves me by what he says and does. Above all, he listens patiently to me. He usually is quite sensitive to my needs—spiritually, mentally, and physically. Lester is always ready to hear my side of any situation, and he's not afraid to admit when he's wrong."

*Dennis, the Encouraging One.* "We have faced a constant financial struggle in the eleven and a half years of our marriage. With three children, we seem to never be able to pay our bills. It is a real struggle for me to remain unaffected when we don't have enough money to meet our obligations. Dennis, however, reminds me not to worry, because worry always makes things worse. Sure enough, we do somehow (with God's help) scratch together the money. Because Dennis has such a good attitude—and it rubs off on me—I feel my life is in God's hands."

*Forgiveness Helps a Lot.* "My husband's willingness to forgive and forget makes it easier for me to pick up the pieces and try again when I know I've failed. I can't remember any time in our almost nine years of marriage when he retaliated—or even mentioned some mistake I made. It's wonderful to have a husband who forgives instead of retaliating."

*Ready to Compliment.* "My husband gives me sincere compliments. Not a day goes by that I don't receive a compliment. I tend to minimize my abilities, so it's easy to see why I find his compliments so welcome and uplifting."

*Robert Helps Me Relax.* "Robert is easygoing. He calls me 'Martha' because Martha was the busy one, always doing something. Robert often says, 'Slow down—sit down for a while and relax.' That's not easy to do with four little kids running helter-skelter, but I certainly need to hear it from him. I'm relieved that my feelings and opinions are important to him, and that he lets me air them and then takes them seriously."

*My Feelings and Opinions Count.* "My husband lets me speak my mind. Sometimes I don't like the way he reacts, but I feel free to say what I wish."

*He Doesn't Demand.* "My husband is not a demanding person. Don't get me wrong—he likes cooked meals, clean clothes, fresh sheets, a tidy house, well-kept children, and a wife he can be proud of, but he doesn't demand these things. He loves them into existence.

"Not once in our eight years of marriage has he insisted that his home is his castle or that he has to have his life a certain way. As we began raising our family and buying a house, he continually told me how much the things I did for him and the boys mattered. All that made me want to do them all the more."

*Paul Isn't Pushy.* "Paul loves me the way I am. I know there are things he would be glad to see changed, but he never pushes. He accepts me as I am, and that makes me want to please him. If I felt he was out to change me, I know I'd prop my feet and feel badly about my own worth."

*Dave Is Dependable.* "What makes Dave easy to live with is that he assumes responsibility. I can depend on him to follow through on his promises. Having a responsible husband takes away a lot of my worry and concern."

*He Has Time to Talk.* "When I have been home alone all day with small duties, I need to have time to talk. When my husband comes home, he wants to talk about his day and hear about mine. That is a really good time! We often hear about wives who talk too much, but I pity wives whose husbands talk too little."

**For further thought for wives:**
> *How would you describe in one paragraph what makes your husband easy to live with?*

# 6.
# *What Makes My Wife Easy to Live With*

Husbands had their chance to answer the question, "What makes your wife easy to live with?" Here are answers, representative of the many that were offered.

*Patience.* "My wife has patience when mine grows thin. Pat has taught me how to be more tolerant. Also, she helps me to slow down when the going is tough and I am inclined to act hastily. She has, I'm sure, saved my face in many situations and also saved many situations."

*Wide Interests.* "In spite of being a mother of four children, my wife keeps alert to world and community happenings. I enjoy hearing her discuss current subjects. She is a lover of books, and her insights are always stimulating."

*A Kind of Thermostat.* "My wife is a kind of thermostat in our home. She listens so well and knows how to make genuinely positive comments. In that way she sets the temperature of the family. I can be quite discouraged, and she always seems to be able to see something good, or she sees how things might work out okay. Her spirit makes her not only easy to live with, but makes life easier to live."

*Joy Pervades Her Life.* "The first thing that comes to my mind is that my wife enjoys keeping things running at home. It's really fun living with a person who loves to make others happy."

*Sharing and Caring Love.* "My wife is a sharing person. She gives herself to others. Her care and concern are visible in the ways she deals with our children. She listens attentively to them. Such a person is easy to live with. I am very touched by her caring love with the children."

*Puts Up with My Grouchiness.* "My wife seems able a lot of times to absorb my grouchiness with patience and understanding. When I am tired and ready to complain, she has a way of encouraging me. Her uplifting words are always there. They move me onward and upward in whatever I'm doing."

*Accepts Me.* "From the time we first met, my wife has accepted me just for being me. It doesn't depend on what I say or do. I'm the silent type, and she accepts me as such. It's the best feeling of all just to be accepted and loved because I am who I am. And so I don't worry about being rejected. Even if I don't get the painting done or some of my other work finished, she loves me."

*Receives Others.* "My wife willingly receives friends, guests, and even an occasional drifter. Bev enjoys doing things for others."

*Accepts.* "Ann doesn't try to change me into some ideal she may have. She allows me to talk about problems that concern me without telling me not to feel that way. By accepting me and listening without reprimanding me, she allows me time to think through situations. I need that."

*Spends Wisely.* "My wife uses our money wisely. She can spot a bargain, doesn't spend needlessly, and knows the value of different kinds of food, clothes, and other needs a family has. I do not know how I'd face a lot of debts or deal with the situation if I were married to a spendthrift. I can thank her for a balanced budget."

*Gives Love Away.* "On the wall in our house hangs a plaque with the statement, 'Love is not love until it is given

away.' My wife, Nancy, knows how to give love. She over-
looks my faults and looks for the best. Early in our marriage we struggled over small irritations, but we've learned
to work through them because my wife gave away such
love."

*Enjoys My Company.* "My wife enjoys my company.
When I work late at night, she usually waits to eat with me.
Instead of complaining about my being late and causing her
extra work, which my schedule often does, she makes our
time together especially meaningful."

*I Feel Needed.* "My wife makes me feel needed. She does
it by the way she consults me and the way we talk over decisions. She wants to know my opinion. Actually, the more I
feel needed, the more I feel my need for her. She has a way
of making everyone she meets feel important."

*Connie is Confidential.* "My wife is not a gossip, and I
know she's careful about what she tells others. Connie can
keep a secret, and it is comforting to know I can share anything with her. Others also must sense this, because many
persons talk to her about their personal problems."

**For further thought for husbands:**
> *How would you describe in one paragraph what
> makes your wife easy to live with?*

# 7.
# Love, Respect, and Submission

So much language about love is full of clichés. Every season there are new love songs about dating, courtship, and marriage. Even the traditional wedding vows have become so commonplace that one wonders if the persons saying them understand their promises to love and take each other for better or for worse, for richer or for poorer, in sickness or in health, until death parts.

No one actively suggests that we should stick it out only as long as we feel love, or only if everything goes perfectly, or only if our spouse turns out to have no faults. We know that love is not a mere feeling. Love is a way of acting. We decide and promise to do what love would do in all circumstances of life together. But we often fail in our commitments because we haven't allowed ourselves to face what such a commitment truly means.

In Ephesians 5 an active love relationship is described. There are four major ways in which this love behaves.

First, we are to love to the point of self-sacrifice. Just like Christ loved the church and gave himself for all of us, so each of us is to love our spouse. This is a strange language in a time of "Me-itis," when many professional counselors and society in general advocates, "I must be me" and "I must look out for myself first of all." Yet it will always be true that a marriage cannot be happy, and it will not last, without the sacrifice of self.

Second, we are to love each other so fully that we have a

pure love life together. As Christ lived purely for all our sakes, so we are to live pure lives out of love for each other. If we are each to love our spouse truly, we will not let our eyes and heart wander to the illicit or the impure—whether it be in magazines, books, movies, or other relationships which lead to wrong thoughts and actions.

A mother sat down with her son who was about to be married. She told me that she urged him to "Keep your eyes for your wife. God has made your father's eyes grow old along with me so that I am still beautiful in his sight."

Third, we ought to let our love be full of positive care and concern. Just like we take care of our bodies, we are to care for the welfare and the emotional, spiritual, and physical health of our spouse. If one of our fingers is hurt, we do all we can to help it heal. So we should care for the happiness and well-being of our spouse.

Fourth, we are to love in a way that maintains our separation and our unity. In every wedding sermon I give I explain what marriage means, both to the couple getting married and to those who attend the wedding— "Marriage means that you have ceased looking for any other marriage or sex partner." That's what we pledge before the community of faith and friends who gather at a wedding. I have found the person with whom I promise to spend the rest of my life, and I will no longer allow myself to look for another possible person. This decision has many meaningful consequences for marital happiness.

Further along, the scripture urges spouses to respect each other. For love cannot grow without respect.

I am concluding, from my years of counseling, writing, teaching, and speaking about the husband-wife relationship, that the area in which husbands need to be most alert is to express a tender, caring, and true love for their wives. Wives should be especially careful to show a deep, abiding, and evident respect for their husbands.

After a session about the meaning of Christian marriage, a woman in her sixties approached me. "I have known for a long time that love is a commitment. It means we act lovingly even if we don't always feel like it. But only today did I come to realize that the same is true of respect. I can demonstrate respect for my spouse, even if at times I feel there is little to respect."

When we love, we make each other lovable; when we honor, we make each other honorable; when we respect, we make each other respectable. We ought to commit ourselves to doing that.

The Bible speaks to both husband and wife in Ephesians 5:21. "Be in submission to one another out of reverence for Christ." That statement surely surprised those who heard it first in biblical times. It was written at a time when women were little more than chattels and when men dominated all society. Yet God's word was that men should practice submission to their wives, and wives should practice submission to their husbands.

This is not cowing down, lording over, or exercising control. Rather, it is yielding to that which is good for each other. It involves a compromising spirit without which no marriage can exist. It means to have such love for each other and such respect for the head of the home, Christ himself, that there is a tender, willing yieldedness to each other.

Only the weak are stubborn, unyielding, and domineering. The strong are those who know the worth and the power of submitting to each other.

**For further thought:**
> *Are the terms "love," "respect," and "submit" positive terms to you?*

# VII.

## Revel
## in the
## Goodness
## and
## Beauty
## of Sex

# VII.

## Revel
## in the
## Goodness
## and
## Beauty
## of Sex

# 1.
## Sex—A Sensitive Thermometer

Some years ago, while speaking to approximately a thousand leaders of the Marriage Encounter movement, I offered an observation which seemed to catch their imaginations. "Sex is a sensitive thermometer telling the temperature of a marriage."

This statement is exactly opposite of what we are led to believe by the soaps, the movies, and the many books and magazine articles about love and sex. Their point-of-view seems to be, "If your sex is good in your marriage, then your marriage is great."

But I believe that if other aspects of one's marriage are great, sex will likely be meaningful and fulfilling, and even exciting. That is, if both husband and wife have a deep sense of being loved, accepted, and appreciated by the other, there is little question that their sexual life will be a cherished and fulfilling experience. If spouses are communicating well in other aspects of their marriage, their sexual communication is nearly assured. But if spouses do not sense love and acceptance in their relationship, and if they do not communicate in depth about their feelings and ideas, it is doubtful that they will have a meaningful sex experience.

Each of us brings our own background and particular understandings to our sexual life. One perceptive cartoonist drew a newly married couple in bed with pictures of their parents looking down upon them disapprovingly.

Some persons come from homes in which talking about sex was taboo, ignored, considered perverted, or even punished. A couple can overcome such mistaken concepts by talking freely and openly about the feelings and attitudes they each bring to their marriage.

Sexual intercourse establishes what the Bible describes as becoming "one flesh." This is not a casual union or simply a union of two bodies. Each of us brings our body, but also our soul, spirit, and mind. And when two people give themselves to each other in the privacy and sanctity of this marital bond, their union is more than merely body to body. It is the profound joining together of mind to mind, heart to heart, and soul to soul.

Sexual intercourse is a mystery reserved for the sacred and God-given relationship of marriage. When a woman and a man each leave their parents, cleave to each other, and become one flesh, they are committing themselves to not hiding any parts of their minds, hearts, souls, spirits, or bodies from each other.

To join bodies in a "one-flesh" union is a great mystery to be reserved, anticipated, celebrated, and enjoyed by those who have committed all they are to each other in order to know all of each other. It is through the body that we express who we are as co-equal sexual beings.

The Hebrew word for coitus or intercourse is the word *yada*, which is translated "to know." We discover more about our own masculinity and femininity through intercourse—and we gain a more intimate knowledge of our spouse in all other levels of life. It allows a husband and wife to know each other as each has never known another. Intercourse allows each of us to unveil ourselves to our spouse so that we may each communicate with the other at the deepest levels of life; in fact, at all levels of life.

This makes the relationship of husband and wife closer

than any other relationship in life. It is closer than a parent and child. This is why a sexual relationship is cherished and protected and reserved for only marriage partners. To share such a relationship beyond marriage is to prostitute it. "You shall not commit adultery" is God saying, "Do not take this gift I've given you and give it to anyone else." Doing so is to despise the gift and to disintegrate and fragment life at the deepest levels we humans can know.

Sexuality is power. Sadly, some persons use their sexuality as others use money or authority. Sexual power plays usually grow out of feeling insecure. It is devastating for a marriage if partners use sex to get their way or to punish the other—that is, if they use sex as a weapon or a reward.

Sex is not something which results only in the birth of a child. Sex is not something to be demanded as a right. It is not meant to be withheld in anger or taken in lust.

Sexual adjustment and satisfaction do not usually come automatically to a couple. At first, intercourse is often awkward, and anxiety adds to the difficulty. No duet is perfect at its first practice. But with patience and practice, harmony can be realized.

Sexual fulfillment is directly related to the whole range of our feelings for each other. If we enjoy each other as persons and joyfully meet each other's needs in other areas of life, we are likely to have a sexual relationship that is warm and strong. The level at which we experience mutual sexual satisfaction is likely an index to how well we are communicating, caring, being honest, enjoying, and experiencing freedom with each other.

**For further thought:**
> *Do you think couples can meet each other's needs sexually if they are not meeting each other's needs in other parts of life?*

# 2.
# *Intended for Intimacy*

"And God said, 'It is not good for man to be alone; I will make a help fit for him'" (Genesis 2:18, RSV).

God created us with a need and a wish for intimacy. Intimacy is the inner sense of closeness which makes us feel as though we belong. We feel accepted as we are, we feel understood, we feel loved. Intimacy involves a kind of sensitivity which moves us toward more and more communion with another. Each of us longs for this kind of relationship.

Genesis 2 lists loneliness as one of the primary problems of life. God recognized this as a serious need and provided a partner for Adam with whom he could share at every level. When a husband and wife experience such closeness, they are discovering a gift from God. And through such human intimacy, they gain a greater understanding of God.

Intimacy takes time. It means being willing to let another enter your inner world. It means expressing your most hidden life currents. Intimacy can bring caring and comfort. It can release you from fears, phobias, and frustrations which otherwise hinder happiness.

Gibson Winter in *Love and Conflict* says that "an intimate relationship is a bond of mutual concern and support between equals. Two people stand together as equals in their concern for another. No distinctions of ability, mental aptitude, riches, or office can be allowed to dominate an intimate relationship. These barriers may exist in other settings, but they cannot be allowed to operate in friendship or marriage. Barriers of inequality are excluded from consideration in intimate relationships. Persons built together by mutual love and concerns exist for one another. Each will help the other and support the other. They counsel one another in difficulty and rescue one another in danger. These are the qualities of an intimate relationship."

Intimacy is destroyed by selfishness, manipulation, and a drive to control, all of which lead to anger and alienation. When we try to restrict rather than release each other, we react in resistance instead of intimacy. When we aim to mold each other rather than unfold each other, we end up with negative reaction and hostility instead of drawing close in love and care.

If I experience loneliness or lack of intimacy in my marriage, I am very likely to develop deep fears, anxiety, and mistrust. Such feelings of isolation are accompanied by a sense of rejection and uselessness. Loneliness often leads a person to latch onto another person or group which appears accepting. And in finding even a little acceptance, a lonely person is likely to lose all sense of discrimination. It is natural for a person to choose nearly any kind of condition or relationship over loneliness.

So a marriage which lacks a growing intimacy is in real danger. When partners suffer growing loneliness, they can easily become involved in all kinds of wrong relationships, illnesses, phobias, and bitterness.

We can know true intimacy only in the safety of complete commitment, only when we accept each other fully as we are, when we include and consider each other in our thoughts and plans, when we seek to understand each other even though we are different and may disagree, when we share as fully as possible through the way we treat and talk to each other.

Commitment is essential because intimacy involves more than talking. Intimacy is an invitation to share in the mystery of each other at the deepest levels. Intimacy needs to be nurtured and encouraged. Spouses who truly wish for intimacy need to commit themselves to interact, to give and to receive at all possible levels. The reward of intimacy is the realization that we are no longer alone in life, that we have someone special to return to and to have return to us.

When my own basic need for growing intimacy is satisfied, I am able to feel and know how special my spouse is. We can begin to experience the freedom of opening the secret places of our lives as we live together. Someone who cares for me is able to offer me acceptance, nonjudgmental support, and the embrace that I cannot supply for myself. When we experience such intimacy, we find it is worth far more than the vulnerability we risk to achieve intimacy.

Such knowledge of the secret recesses of my partner's life, thoughts, and feelings creates a bond of endearment and enduring strength. We are sure of each other's love; we can count on the security of each other's commitment to stand side-by-side, regardless of what may come into our marriage. We become, as the experience has been aptly described, persons "to whom we can turn, knowing that being with them is coming home."

**For further thought:**

> *Do you agree that true intimacy can be expressed only in the safety of complete commitment and acceptance?*

# 3.
# *Intimacy Is Enhanced*

"Open your hearts to one another and God will be glorified" (Romans 15:7, Phillips).

How do we grow in intimacy? How do we fulfill this deep longing we bring to our marriages to each know our partner in greater and greater depths of love? We have learned to know and appreciate each other because we developed a growing intimacy before we were married. How do we enter the unending possibilities of becoming a greater resource to each other in every way as we experience love, acceptance, understanding, and support, now that we are married?

We nurture intimate relationships by honestly and lovingly trying to share feelings. We may be tempted to hide our honest feelings because we're afraid that our spouse, whose care we covet, may not love and accept us. But doing that puts such severe restraints on our relationship that it will dry up and die.

To hide from each other is to put up a false front, frustrate intimacy, and foster mistrust. Not only that, if we fail to share our feelings, we will use our energies to defend ourselves rather than reveal ourselves. And our greatest gifts and love will not be shared. Only as we are willing to open our hearts to each other, honestly and gently, will we be able to identify what we want to share and where we need to negotiate and grow.

We enhance intimacy if we are close physically. Touching

is healing, comforting, reassuring, and caring. Touching adds to our physical and emotional well-being. Loving touches can lead to meaningful sexual intercourse. In fact, without such caring touching, a couple's sexual relationship can lose meaning.

A couple can increase their intimacy by looking into each other's eyes. Why not pledge to look into your spouse's eyes each day? Something happens when husbands and wives do that. This simple practice has become an essential part of marriage enrichment programs. One couple described the deep spiritual experience they had when they prayed for each other while looking into each other's eyes.

To build intimacy we need to commit to use the full range of our senses—touch, sight, facial expressions, and speech—in a warm and responsible way.

Intimacy grows as we explore ideas, share experiences of beauty, create together, have fun, work at common tasks, cope with problems, face pain, and struggle together over our differences. We grow together when we commit ourselves to common goals and when we promise to express our inner fears and struggles, our temptations and our joys, our despair as well as our delight; when we say what pains us in our relationship, as well as what gives us pleasure.

Let me state a word of caution. Such intimacy presumes a sacred circle of privacy around the couple which both spouses must preserve. No one else has any right to come within that sacred circle. Partners may not share with others the inadequacies of their spouses.

All of us have heard sad stories from those who have compared notes about the relative adequacy of their husband or wife as lovers. This can only be demoralizing and self-defeating. While marital difficulties may, at times, be shared beneficially by a spouse with a competent counselor, intimacy can easily be destroyed by indiscriminate sharing of even small matters. Intimacy needs confidence and trust to grow.

Many marriages enjoy little spiritual intimacy, even though it is the basis of all true intimacy. Psychiatrist Paul Tournier in *Marriages That Work* describes the level of intimacy he and his wife Nelly experienced when they learned, after difficult early years of struggle, to share in prayer, Bible reading, and spiritual encouragement. "We became," he says, "confessors for each other" and experienced great healing and blessing.

There is no limit to intimacy in marriage. As we open our hearts, express our thoughts, give our bodies, and release our very souls to each other, we find it true as Erasmus said centuries ago: "The wedlock of mind will be greater than the wedlock of bodies."

**For further thought:**
> *What do you see as the greatest builders or the greatest destroyers of intimacy?*

# 4.
## What Is Sexual Success?

Sexual success is a preoccupation for many persons. But what do they think sexual success is? Sexual expectations are set by advertisers, by the affairs portrayed in soap operas, by scandalous literature, movies, plays, and television. Most of these standards are filled with fantasy, falsehood, and infidelity. They will not lead to meaningful sex.

Even the information about sex which comes from so-called experts is frequently based on reports of people with unsatisfactory experiences, sick marriages, and illicit relationships.

This stress on the negative takes attention away from what is needed for a sexual relationship to have real meaning, pleasure, and fulfillment. The primary focus must always be on having a loving relationship in other areas of life if sexual intercourse is to have pleasure and purpose and to be all God intends it to be.

In his fine book *Whom God Hath Joined*, David R. Mace writes, "We often talk about sexual intercourse as 'making love.' Strictly speaking, that is not true. The meeting of two bodies cannot make love. It can only express and enrich a love that is already there. And the quality of the experience will depend upon the quality of love that it expresses."

When things go wrong with sex, the problem is usually not sex. Problems with sex most often come when spouses have other problems that need attention.

Sex is important in a marriage. Loving marriage partners make sex satisfying and meaningful. It is obvious that persons can engage in sex without loving each other. But the richness which blends both spirits and bodies and which binds two people in greater oneness can be realized only as the result of deep trust, respect, admiration, and freedom—all characteristics of true love.

The Scriptures consider sexual communion as a deeply significant symbol of sharing life at many levels. Sexual problems are usually symptoms of trouble elsewhere in a marriage. Making a satisfying sexual adjustment is usually not difficult for a couple who are eager to please each other. There is usually a satisfying solution when there is sympathetic understanding.

John L. Thomas, S.J., a noted sociologist who has written widely on the subject of marriage, says concerning sex and healthy marriages, "But it's the totality of reality that people should be concerned with, not just a small part, especially in dealing with human relationships. If a person has not been able to come to terms with life, or find meaning or significance in it generally, he's not likely to find them [meaning or significance] in any part of it. It will all, including sex, then, seem monotonous and drab."

Sexual fulfillment does not mean measuring up to some description we have read in a book or to some experience we have seen portrayed in a movie. It does grow out of warmth and freedom in the whole range of our feelings for our spouse. It means enjoying each other as persons and joyfully meeting each other's needs in every area of life. The level at which we experience mutual satisfaction is the level at which we are communicating, caring, being honest, enjoying, and experiencing freedom in the many parts of our marriage relationship.

**For further thought:**

> *What images of sexual success or expectations did you bring to marriage?*

# 5.
# *Unity Expressed in Sex*

Our sexual experience as husband and wife reveals much about our relationship in general. The unity we sense in sexual intimacy stems from how united we are in other things. Our openness and honesty in sexual relations tell how open and honest we are in the rest of life together. The way we communicate our feelings in sex is closely related to the kind of communication we experience in all parts of our marriage.

The love we feel in sexual intercourse flows from the love we express and feel throughout the day. The joy we experience in this most intimate relationship is the result of the joy we find in the presence of each other at other times. The satisfaction of sexual intimacy corresponds to the satisfaction we experience as partners in all of life.

Therefore, if we desire oneness, openness, communication, trust, and feelings of love, joy, and satisfaction in sexual intercourse, we must practice bringing these qualities to the full range of our relationship as husband and wife. Sexual intimacy will then heighten and confirm these qualities.

Life's purpose for married partners is not all passion and ecstasy. Most of marriage is made up of everyday, mundane chores. So the only way to live happy lives is to invest our common tasks with quality. Then they will become sources and expressions of sexual intimacy.

We should keep in mind that sex is God's creation, and

that it is good, pure, right, and to be enjoyed in marriage. So we should be able to talk about sex freely and frankly until we no longer have attitudes of hesitancy and fear or shame and guilt. Otherwise, our relationship will suffer. We want to invest our sexual relations with all the pleasure we can; we want to do and say whatever makes sex as enjoyable as possible for each other.

If we were starting our marriage again, we would realize that sex is one of the primary ways we express our love for each other and meet each other's needs. It is a grave mistake to withhold sex to retaliate against or control the other. That kind of practice brings serious repercussions; it builds hostility and tears a marriage into shreds.

Scripture is surprisingly clear about this: "The husband should give to his wife her conjugal rights, and likewise the wife to her husband . . . Do not refuse one another except perhaps by agreement for a season, that you may devote yourselves to prayer; but then come together again, lest Satan tempt you through lack of self control" (I Corinthians 7:3,5 RSV).

The point is plain. We should not withhold sexual love from each other. Not only does that undermine trust and companionship, it can severely tempt partners to be unfaithful.

For a husband and wife to understand and satisfy each other, they must communicate. They must express their feelings and needs. They must say what gives pleasure and what hinders their sexual fulfillment. The greater their freedom to express love, feelings, and needs, the greater their satisfaction and joy.

When I discuss sexual adjustment in premarital counseling, I always stress that a couple will save themselves much pain and many adjustment problems if they are completely open with each other from the start about what gives sexual satisfaction and what each spouse would like the other to do.

It is strange how we keep each other in the dark about this, all the while expecting the other to know our wishes and often getting quietly upset because the other isn't meeting our needs.

We come together as two very different persons sexually. How can we know each other's needs unless we express them? A man has little idea about what is most delightful to his wife unless she tells him. A wife wants her husband to tell her his wishes.

The ability to communicate openly, honestly, and frankly in this most intimate area gets a couple off to a good start in adjusting to marriage. And the feelings of closeness and oneness that result only contribute to a happy and exciting sexual experience.

What is permissible in marital sex? Anything which satisfies both, which meets the deepest needs of both. When one of the partners is not satisfied or feels violated, sex is no longer the great experience God intended, nor that for which we all long.

### For further thought:

> *If you were starting your marriage over again, what advice about sex would you give to a newly married couple?*

# 6.
# Patience and Practice

First efforts at sexual intercourse are seldom skillful or satisfying. Some say that fewer than fifty percent of couples experience initial satisfaction. For ten percent, it may take twenty years or more. Whatever a couple's progress, when love, honesty, and concern are present, they can still know an inner sense of pleasure and oneness.

No amount of factual knowledge can bring lasting satisfaction to sex if we do not love each other. Satisfying sex depends more upon kindness, courtesy, openness, and consideration than upon skill and knowledge.

When we approach sex with the attitude of giving happiness and pleasure, and seeking to meet the needs of our partner, we find joy returned and our own needs met. When both find fulfillment and renewal, sex is good, and a couple's unity and love are strengthened.

One writer defines sexual intimacy without interpersonal intimacy as having a diploma without an education—an apparent achievement with no real substance behind it. How can we express love in bed if we don't take time to cultivate love outside of bed? With loving kisses, words, hugs, and touches during the day, we add to the delight of sexual union. When we love someone, we want that person to be satisfied. When we care for another, we supply and guard that person's welfare. When we are part of a truthful and trustful relationship, we each have the freedom to express fully what produces the most pleasure and what hinders enjoyment. Love is the over-arching quality that makes it all possible. As Harry Stack Sullivan said years ago, "When the satisfaction or the security of another person becomes as significant to one as one's own satisfaction or security, then a state of love exists."

The sexual area of married love cannot be ignored if a marriage is to be happy. In other areas of married life a couple can disagree and yet live happily. Here, because our biology brings us together, we must either deal with our problems and differences or settle for an unsatisfactory sexual and marital experience.

We dare not allow this important love expression to be crowded into hurried moments or hours of fatigue. Sex, to be enjoyed, needs plenty of time, so that a couple can relax in each other's arms. It is easy to become so occupied with living that we don't have time for loving.

Sex develops a special, individual meaning for each couple. Sexual intimacy is fed by love and feeds love. A key part of married happiness is the exhilarating joy of sexual love.

**For further thought:**
> *How can couples deal with the common but false expectations that sexual satisfaction will be instantaneous?*

# 7.
# Covenant of Fidelity

George E. Sweazy in *In Holy Matrimony* writes, ". . . the final, bodily giving of a man and woman to each other is intended by God and by their natures to express the complete and permanent giving of their whole selves. Without this it is a dishonest symbol, an enacted lie. They cannot give themselves in this way to more than one person; it cannot be for a limited time. This commitment must be complete."

The covenant of fidelity rises naturally out of the standard of monogamy that is taught in Genesis and referred to in every major discussion of marriage in the Scriptures. The deep and intimate and personal oneness of marriage excludes a third party or sharing acts of intimacy with anyone else.

The traditional wedding vows are absolute. We promise to take each other only, to forsake all others, to leave and to cleave and to keep only to each other as long as we both shall live.

Edith Dean says, "Marriage, as ordained by the Creator, upheld by Jesus, and taught by Christian leaders like Paul, is monogamous. It is the most personal and cherished of all human relationships. In such a union the noblest and best relationship between a man and a woman is formed. A family composed of a husband and wife who love each other, and of children conceived in their love, is the first and oldest, as well as the holiest and greatest, human institution."

Notice that when Jesus speaks about marriage he begins not in the realm of action, but in the area of attitudes and thoughts. "You have heard that it was said . . . you shall not commit adultery: but I say unto you, that whosoever looks on a woman to lust after her has committed adultery with her already in his heart" (Matthew 5:27-28).

Jesus, knowing human nature, points to the fact that before open unfaithfulness, there is a time of secret disloyalty in thought. Lusting—the desire for that which is wrong—prepares the way for the act of adultery.

We must be continually alert about this. Lust is encouraged all around us in magazines, movies, dress and undress, loose talk, and a general obsession with sex and adultery. Soap operas, built on infidelity and impurity, are present at the turn of a dial. People who would not permit pornographic magazines in their homes allow these subtle suggestions in their living rooms through TV. Persons committed to fidelity in marriage will avoid these images.

Three great fundamental truths are from the Bible. First, God never intended a sexual relationship to be temporary. It is permanent. A satisfactory sexual experience does not exist apart from the life partnership of one man and one woman. "Eros" love makes others objects of passion and selfishly says, "Please me!" "Agape" love, which God intends, makes another person the object of our deepest love and looks to protect and please the other.

Second, we must guard against being unfaithful in our thinking and our actions. Refuse to imagine sexual relationships which would violate marriage—our own or someone else's. This demands that we are loyal in every area of our marital relationship. We are loyal to our spouse over family and friends; we express our loyalty in the way we use our money and other things that we own. We are loyal in how we talk about each other to others and in the time we take for each other.

Jesus did not mean that we should not admire a beautiful person or that we should deny our sexual feelings. To be faithful to our mate does not mean that we are prudish or stiff with ourselves or the opposite sex. A proper appreciation of the feminine can add to a man's warm relationship with his wife; a woman who properly appreciates the masculine can have an enhanced relationship with her husband. But to let our minds dwell on the illicit is an altogether different thing and is the first step to infidelity.

Third, premarital and extramarital sex are not only unsatisfactory; they are wrong. "Thou shalt not commit adultery" is placed next to "Thou shalt not murder" in the Ten Commandments. God's intent is to protect the total personality, the very life of each marriage partner. The idea of infidelity is revolting and remote to the minds of true lovers. It violates all that is good—security, acceptance, and love. The New Testament is equally clear: "Do not be deceived: neither the sexually immoral nor idolaters, nor adulterers, nor male prostitutes, nor homosexual offenders, nor thieves, not the greedy, nor drunkards, nor slanderers, nor swindlers will inherit the kingdom of God" (I Corinthians 6:9, 10).

"Marriage should be honored by all, and the marriage bed kept pure, for God will judge the adulterer and all the sexually immoral" (Hebrews 13:4).

This may sound old-fashioned in our atmosphere of sexual freedom. But time has proven that the only way life and marriage work is by being faithful to one's spouse. Marriage must have the covenant of fidelity.

**For further thought:**

> Are people who are promiscuous unable to find true satisfaction in sex? Is their continual search related to the fact that sexual happiness can be satisfied only in a faithful relationship?

# VIII.

# Be Faithful in Little Things

# 1.
# Don't Try
# to Change Each Other

After the honeymoon, the new husband asked his bride, "Honey, you don't mind if I point out a few faults you have, do you?"

"Absolutely not," replied the young wife. "It's those faults which kept me from getting a better husband, dear."

"What have you learned these days together?" I asked a group of couples at the final session of a Marriage Enrichment seminar. A wife, with tears in her eyes, had an immediate response. "What I have learned is that I must stop trying to change Bill. I've tried for twenty-five years to change him. And it hasn't worked one bit. I see what I need to do is love and accept him."

If this wife learned that lesson, she was well on the way to a happy marriage. Her husband, sitting by her side, was a fine person, loved by all of us there. Yet they had struggled for years because, in this instance, the wife sought to change rather than love and accept.

One of the early and chief temptations many marriages face is when one or both partners tries to become Creator all over again and aims to create the other into his or her own image. Sometimes the struggle starts in courtship. Sometimes it starts soon after the wedding vows. But whenever we try to change each other we are headed for hostility, trouble, and reaction. Then the opposite sex becomes the opposition sex. When we try to change each other rather than accept each other, we say, "You are unsatisfactory." When we feel pressure to change, we respond with resistance and dig in our heels. Married life becomes an endless duel rather than an enjoyable duet.

One area in which Betty and I have had many hard feelings and difficulties is the matter of arriving at appointments and events on time. Early on we learned that one of us is prompt, while the other is not as time-conscious. Again and again we got upset with each other at the very time we should have been feeling especially good toward each other. Here we were, leaving for a church service to speak about love or starting out for a husband/wife retreat which we were to conduct, and we were angry with each other because we were late again. That is not conducive to anything good!

We've worked hard at this problem, and, for the most part, succeeded in reducing the friction a great deal. We decided we have too many meetings to convene and too many schedules to keep to let such a habit handicap us. We decided to work at it together, and so we try to help each other get ready in good time and plan ahead to avoid a mad rush.

A nervous bride asked her pastor how to deal with the anxiety she felt about the wedding service. The pastor gave her a surefire formula. "As you come through the door keep your eyes down," he advised her. "Don't look around at the people. Keep your gaze fixed on the aisle where you will walk. Then when you are about halfway down the aisle, raise your eyes just a bit until you see the altar. Keep your eyes fastened there until you are nearly to the front. Finally, look up just the slightest bit until you see him—your beloved."

The day of the wedding came. The church was full. The

"Wedding March" began. The doors opened and there stood the beautiful young bride looking remarkably composed. People did wonder, however, about what she muttered determinedly under her breath as she passed by: "Aisle, alter, him. Aisle, alter, him." Many young brides marry with the intention that "I'll alter him." Unfortunately it rarely works.

Learning to love and accept each other is one of the biggest jobs we have—and one which also carries some of the richest rewards.

**For further thought:**

*In what areas have you struggled or tried to change each other?*

# 2.
# *What We Remember*

Our friends' TV wasn't working. They turned the dials and checked the fuse box. One of them kicked it a little thinking that a jolt might turn it on. Finally they called a repair person who noticed the thing was unplugged. No one thought to check that!

"Whenever something isn't working," the repair person told the family, "check the small and simple things first. Ninety-nine percent of troubles are with the small things."

We have found it's the little things which make or break a marriage. Many of us can manage enough muscle to handle the major things in life—accidents, financial difficulty, and even death. Often when a marriage fails, it is because the partners didn't practice little kindnesses or use considerate words of love. Small deeds and thoughtful words add luster and joy to love. Their absence lets coldness creep in. Neglecting love little by little becomes a tremendous collection of trifles which let two lovers drift apart.

As we reflect on our marriage, we can't think of many big things that we did to care for our marriage. But we do remember the encouraging words we said to each other during times of stress and difficulty, the times we relaxed together by heading to some quiet place, and the cards and small gifts we gave at unexpected times.

We have created a ritual with our children around a special cup which we call "the family cup." We looked a long time for the cup. Finally, a good friend who knew about our search gave us a tall, communion-like cup. We don't use it at all as a regular cup. Rather, we have a ceremony in which it becomes a simple symbol of our family unity. When our family passes the cup around the table, and each child and parent drinks from it and then expresses love and appreciation for the others, it enlarges our love. Passing the cup is a small symbolic act, but it has helped us to build loving and caring relationships and to create a sense of unity.

We remember joining hands around the table, praying for one another, and thanking God for many blessings. We remember long walks, hand-in-hand. We remember touching each other while driving along in the car. We remember praying for the safety of others and ourselves as we traveled, and for a happy time together. These are little things, but they take on significant size as we look back.

I try to remember to pray each day, "Lord, make me great in little things." The small things of life make us—and those we love—sad and glad.

Think of all the little things you do remember. "I'm sorry," "Excuse me," "Let me help you"—even "Please" and "Thank you"—are like love songs set to beautiful music and can be performed by all. Great brilliance, beauty, and intellect can be admired, but they can't dry a tear or mend a broken spirit. Only kindness can do that.

William Hordern explains why telegraph and cable companies spelled out punctuation marks instead of using symbols such as commas, periods, and question marks. A woman traveling in Europe cabled her husband: "Have found wonderful bracelet. Price seventy-five thousand dollars. Okay to buy it?"

Her husband promptly cabled back, "No, price too high." The telegraph operator in transmitting the message missed the signal for the comma. So the wife read the message, "No price too high." She bought the bracelet. Her husband sued the cable company and won.

A comma seems too small to be significant. But it illustrates the truth that small things can make a big difference in life. And much of life is made up of little things.

**For further thought:**

> *What are the little things you remember from your childhood which helped shape your life?*

# 3.
## *Transferred Treasures*

Thomas Carlyle, satirical author and philosopher, found it hard to express his love to his wife, Jane. He had little time for her. After Jane's death in 1866, Carlyle was sorrowfully going through her belongings when he discovered a diary. He sat down to read what she had written. On many of the pages he noticed that the ink was blurred. When he read more closely, he realized that the stains were blurring statements that had a painful theme.

"Oh, if only you would say something nice to me and show that you appreciate what I do for you. I am so hungry for a bit of praise from you."

It was raining when the gruff literary genius made his way to his wife's grave. He knelt on the rain-soaked clay and whispered, "Oh, Jane, would that I had only known." Preoccupied with his own needs and interests, Carlyle failed to communicate love and appreciation to his emotionally starving wife.

Without a sense of appreciation, even our best efforts become drudgery. Without tenderness, life grows tough. Without a spirit of helpfulness, life turns lonely and slides into drudgery. A little help with some chore can make the meanest task a labor of lasting love.

When we take even a bit of time for each other, the rest of our time benefits and feels transformed. For our marriage to have meaning and joyful togetherness, we must be faithful in the small things and not wait for the big occasion to demonstrate our devotion to each other.

It is true as the Scriptures say, "The one who is faithful in a very little is faithful also in much; and he who is dishonest in a very little is dishonest also in much" (Luke 16:10 RSV).

When a marriage seems to suddenly fail, it is not at all sudden. Beneath the surface, partners did not practice faithfulness in small things for a long time.

Robert E. Goodrich in his book *What's It All About?* explains how a hurricane becomes a death-dealing, monstrous thing. How do these fierce storms work their destruction and death? You will notice that the news reports frequently say, "The hurricane was preceded by torrential rains." This is the secret strategy of a hurricane.

Rain precedes the wind by a number of hours. Millions of tiny raindrops drum the earth. When everything is softened, suddenly the wind strikes. And giant trees which could easily bear a storm under normal circumstances are pushed over. Houses and buildings which could have stood much stronger winds suddenly give way because the soil around them was softened.

So the hurricane is a parable. When marriages collapse, their failure is preceded by many small things done or left undone. That causes a deterioration of the soil which is needed to build strong relationships. When some kind of adversity or difficulty comes along, the marriage falls apart.

### For further thought:

*Do you agree that there are no sudden marriage failures? Why?*

# 4.
# Both Are Involved

When a marriage succeeds, two people are involved; when a marriage fails, two people are also involved. My experience in counseling couples confirms again and again for me that separation or divorce is never one-sided, no matter how innocent one party may appear.

The husband may seem to be the victim because his wife is attracted to someone else. But it's likely that his cold, indifferent, or incommunicative spirit, or his not taking time for his wife, contributed to her wandering away.

A husband may expect his wife to be warm and freely available to him sexually without giving her love, tenderness, and time. Should she fall for another man who pays some attention to her, and should she be swept off her feet and let her emotions go astray, it may look as though her husband bears no blame, but that is probably not the full story.

A wife may seem to be a victim when her husband is drawn to another woman. But if she withholds her love and sex, or in other ways is cold and unresponsive to her husband, she is not innocent. When another woman smiles tenderly at him or listens to his worries, he can easily feel excitement because he misses his wife's interest and affirmation.

A husband and wife may throw out threats. Threats of any kind are little daggers and leave open, hard-to-heal wounds. One husband threw his wedding ring across the room when he got mad. One wife threatened divorce when she didn't get her way and when her husband disagreed with her. Such behavior is not only immature and serious because it slashes the spirit of marriage, but it also causes injury and eats away at the fabric of love and fidelity. Even when it heals, it leaves scars and can lead to distance or separation.

I am not meaning to excuse any kind of unfaithfulness. I am simply stating that when there is marital failure, both perhaps are in some way guilty. And both need to humble themselves, admit their own mistakes, and repent. If your heart and interest jump at the thought or sight of someone of the opposite sex who is not your spouse, not all is well in your marriage.

Every marriage has low times. And then there are times when our commitment to God and each other pulls us through to a richer experience than we ever imagined.

Married partners must continue to communicate, to pray, and to take time together. We must keep our loyalties to God, to our family, and finally to work. There will be chaos in the best of marriages if any one of these gets out of order.

Elements of disharmony are present in every marriage. But all marriages have the prospect of success if two people want to make it succeed together.

### For further thought:

> *Is it true that whenever there is marriage success or failure, two people are responsible?*

# 5.
# *Impact on Children*

The little gestures and words of love which we show to our spouses demonstrate daily to our children what the nature of real love is. Some time ago our daughter told us how warm she felt about our family when she saw me bring a fresh rose from the garden on a summer morning for her mother. This was not a big thing, to be sure. But it was a gift of love. An attitude of love and the feelings of love between a father and mother reach out to bless their family and beyond.

Likewise, it is the little things we do and say to our children which prepare them for relationships and love. If we parents wait to demonstrate our love until a special occasion, a big trip, or "When I have time we'll play a game," we will find life passing us by. By then, even these special times will lack a real sense of love. And we will have missed a multitude of other opportunities to show and experience love.

Try not to miss ordinary opportunities. Don't wait until you have a lot of money to take a trip together. Take a run in the park or do some other activity together now. Don't wait to do special things together only during vacation. Watch for ways to make family time special by enjoying the most mundane moments of each day.

Don't wait for birthdays and anniversaries and Christmas to express your love and say how glad you are that God led you together. Be sure to tell each other then.

But more than that, invest many other occasions with time and effort which say, "You are important to me."

M.A. Kelly wrote, "Small kindnesses, small courtesies, small considerations habitually practiced in our social intercourse, give greater charm to the character than the display of great talents and accomplishments."

Julie Carney wrote the familiar words:

Little deeds of kindnesses,

Little words of love

Help to make earth happy

Like the heaven above.

I have found that when I failed to express my love and caring in the details week-to-week, I also missed showing how I really felt in the big opportunities that came my way. When I forgot to express appreciation routinely and with simple words, my effort at big things sounded hollow.

So I am persuaded more than ever that the way to express great love, appreciation, and faithfulness, as well as a growing oneness, is by practicing love and kindness faithfully day to day.

### *For further thought:*

*What commitments are you willing to make to be faithful to your spouse in little things?*

# 6.
## Looking for the Best

A friend of ours told us about the conversation that went on in a women's group which met in her home. The subject was husbands, and one woman after another made negative remarks. Finally the hostess said, "The way it sounds, you're all trying to get rid of your husbands. I'm doing all I can to keep mine!" Might her attitude be the reason she and her husband have a good relationship?

To see the best in each other we need to overlook a lot and recognize that we all have plenty of faults. What matters most is not that we have faults, but what we do with them.

A group of husbands and wives who wanted help in their marriages met once a week for five weeks. In the first session I suggested that during the next five weeks each person should write down each day one thing which they appreciate about their spouses. I thought it would be interesting to see how many could find at least thirty things which they admired or appreciated.

At the second session I asked how their lists were coming. There was silence for a few moments. Then one woman said, "I thought of one thing."

That silence and the one wife's comment said a great deal about why the marriages were in need of new life. Apparently these spouses were not accustomed to looking for the best in each other.

We each need to learn to love our real partner, not the

imaginary partner we dreamed about. It never works when we try to be missionaries to our spouses. It is insultingly arrogant to try to make a person into something that he or she is not. Sometimes it may seem impossible to survive our partner's idiosyncrasies. But we each can if we will, and that is easier than surviving the resistance which results from trying to change the other.

One wife described how difficult and unhappy she felt when she demanded, nagged, and complained. The reason she was so annoyed by her husband, she finally realized, was that she was thinking of herself too much. But with God's help and strength she changed and developed what she calls a "4-A Strategy: accept him, admire him, adapt to him, appreciate him." The same formula can be used by a husband, too!

I have learned that criticism seldom, if ever, helps. Sometimes it is helpful to express how my spouse's behavior makes me feel, but without labeling or lambasting the other. Personal attacks can only cut and leave scars in our relationships.

And I have discovered that a sense of humor helps. When we can laugh at ourselves, we are on the way to a relaxed relationship. We are more able to avoid tension-filled days, the kind that cause friction and sparks whenever we touch.

When we are able to look for the best, we enlarge our love and bring out the best in ourselves and in our spouses.

### For further thought:

*What would you learn if you made a list of the things you appreciate about your spouse? Try jotting down one thing each day for the next thirty days.*

# IX.

# Be
# Faithful
# in
# Finances

# 1.
## *Money Reveals Us*

We made an important decision early in our marriage. A salesman stopped at our house, and before he left we had signed to buy.

After the salesman left, we found out that we each thought the other wanted the item, and so, without talking further, we had bought it. At that moment we promised each other that we would never again buy anything extra and unplanned for without first discussing it and agreeing together. That decision has saved us a lot of pressure and expense. We have successfully avoided all kinds of impulsive buying. We've decided that if a purchase can't wait or doesn't merit discussion, it's probably not worth buying.

Next to failing to spend time together and communicating effectively, money problems cause major disturbances in many marriages. The promise to love and stick together "for richer or for poorer" is among the most difficult for many couples to keep.

Family service agencies report an increase in family conflicts over money. These tensions are by no means problems only for low wage earners. "Most of our families have enough money to meet basic needs; the problem is management," observes Carol Weaverling of Family Consultation Service in Wichita, Kansas.

To begin, we need to adjust to each other in this area because we come from two different family backgrounds. But money problems may also arise from other problems in our marriage.

Couples who immediately accumulate heavy debt may lack inner security, in contrast to more realistic or more stable couples who start by making modest purchases. Those who are less secure may seek respectability by buying what is new, expensive, and impressive.

Couples function best if they deliberately move from using their money as individuals to planning and using their money together. Sometimes newlyweds' expectations are like TV fantasies, including elaborate or sporty cars for each, boats for water skiing, "loaded" stereos and TVs, and a home with a burdensome mortgage. Financial counselors agree that the most treacherous financial pitfall is a standard of living that exceeds one's income.

Manual Scott calls these expectations "Thingafication." Chrysostom centuries ago described it as "being nailed to the things of life." Generations past spoke of it as "keeping up with the Joneses." The Bible calls it covetousness and a mistaken belief that life's meaning can be found in things.

We will save ourselves heartache and problems by believing what Jesus said about this—living a happy life with meaning does not consist in having abundant money or things. In fact, when we try to satisfy ourselves by buying more, or we believe that an increase in income will solve our problems, we are already in trouble.

### For further thought:

> *How similar or dissimilar are your own and your spouses' backgrounds, assumptions about finances, and handling of money?*

# 2.
# *A Higher Commitment*

As Christians we believe that our commitment to God includes our money. It's a sure sign that God does not control our lives if we withhold our bank accounts from God. If we acknowledge God as owner of our time, abilities, energies, and possessions, that perspective affects how we earn, spend, give, and use what we have.

A couple's happiness together is not related to the size of their income. The happiest times in many marriages are those years when a couple struggles hardest together to make a living.

Frequently, one partner finds it easier to work with finances, budgeting, and spending than the other. Recognizing that strength can be a great help. However, it is especially important that neither partner becomes the exclusive monetary manager so that the other partner shuns all financial responsibility. The time may come in every marriage when illness, or even death, prevents the better money manager from doing the job. This is when shared financial knowledge, as well as agreement about expenditures, is valuable.

For financial happiness a husband and wife need an agreement—if not written, at least understood—which states how they will work together in earning, saving, and spending money; what they will give; and how they will avoid impulsive buying—a real problem in many unhappy marriages.

There is great value in having a definite and a shared system for handling the family money that includes a shared spending plan. Dr. Milton Huber's survey of one hundred over-indebted couples in Michigan found that they lacked an understanding or an agreement on who was responsible for what in handling their money. Nearly a third of the couples gave conflicting answers about who was responsible.

In contrast, among other couples who were not over-extended, interviewers found "clear communication on who paid the bills, kept the budget, and so on."

The difference between harmony and heartache is whether we can agree about our purchases and whether we try diligently to keep spending within our income.

One final note may be helpful. It is wise not to think of starting financially where our parents finished. That is financially dangerous. It may also be important not to make major purchases too early in marriage since a couple's tastes may take time to jell. They may discover that after a number of years they know better what they both like.

**For further thought:**
*When do you think most couples get into trouble financially?*

# 3.
# *Life Is Not in Things*

A husband and wife who were separated when they came for counseling said that it was after they built their third house—and each one was bigger and better than the last—that they realized their marriage was in trouble. Many persons consciously or unconsciously choose money and mansions over their marriages, and are forever unhappy. The Bible says, "Better a meal of vegetables where there is love than a fattened calf with hatred" (Proverbs 15:17 NIV).

Tension over money ranks high among the top causes of struggles in marriages. It is a predominant conflict in those marriages which are in the highest income bracket.

The fact is that a good marriage does not depend upon material things—a bigger and more beautiful house, a new car, or the latest in clothes. Few of us are fully satisfied with our incomes, whatever they are, and nearly everyone seems to think their troubles would be over if more money were available. This, of course, is not true.

Robert Hastings points out that money management is not so much a technique as it is an attitude. Attitudes deal with emotions. So managing money involves controlling one's emotions. If we are to control money, we must learn to control ourselves. Undisciplined use of money usually reveals undisciplined persons.

Dewitt L. Miller in *If Two Are to Become One* writes, "It is also worth noting that a couple who keeps accurate accounting of the way their money is spent will, in almost every instance, spend less and spend more wisely than a couple who keeps no accounts."

Money, like fire, is a faithful servant, but it can be a powerful danger. Because of this we must master it.

The more that spouses are able to be open with each other about finances, the more they will experience cooperation and understanding. Children should also be brought along in this effort so that they, too, learn responsibility for helping make ends meet.

From the start of our marriage, our income was low. We lived on a pastor's salary. But we did several things we are very glad about today. Not only did we try to give liberally to God's work, we taught our children to tithe from the first dime they received. In addition, when the children each turned twelve, we gave them small allowances out of which they bought their own clothes. We supplemented that at birthdays and Christmas with larger items like coats or shoes, but the children learned that if they exceeded their allowances, they were spending their future earnings. This practice was basic training in buying wisely and realizing their responsibility for choices. We would certainly do this again.

One teenager griped continually because he felt that his parents were stingy and wouldn't buy him clothes and other things the way his friends' parents did. After his parents sat down with him and explained their income and the family budget, the young man commented, "I didn't know you had to think about all those things. You're pretty good managers."

A spending plan about which the family agrees helps keep tension out of a home.

**For further thought:**
> *Do you agree that the actual amount a couple earns has little to do with frustrations and family fights?*

# 4.
# A Review
# Is Always in Order

We have learned that it is good, from time to time, to review our finances—income and spending, as well as saving and giving. Without doing that, an excellent plan may fail because your income may diminish, costs of certain items are likely to increase radically, and family needs will continually change as children are born and grow older. Circumstances simply do not stay the same over the years.

When money becomes the battleground, there is a good chance that there are problems elsewhere in the relationship. Money is often simply an excuse for releasing stored up resentments. On the other hand, money can also be a means for creating great satisfaction and growing commitment as we work together to use material things in our marriages.

Although some may consider the following figures unrealistic, they may give some guidance from which to work. A financial counselor, who has helped many families over the years, suggests that a couple probably should not spend more than two and a half years' income for a house. A couple should aim to accumulate half a year's income in a reserve fund and should move toward providing two years' income in life insurance or pension funds. Borrowing should be done wisely and only on income-producing or cost-saving items. Diversify assets. Plan to save some money each pay period, and don't miss the blessing of systematically setting aside a portion of your income for giving to charity.

**For further thought:**
> *Discuss ways to keep real estate from crowding out relationships.*

# 5.

# A Personal Testimony

In counseling couples about their marriages, I have been free to talk about my own pilgrimage and the principles Betty and I have tried to live by. Although our choices may not be the answers for everyone, we can say without regrets that we're grateful we made the decisions that we did.

First, we have purposely decided to live simply. A psychologist friend told me that the best psychologists in the country are not counseling people in personal and family problems like he is. The best psychologists are hired by corporations to tell them how to package and stack things in stores to get people to buy what they do not need. No one, in contrast, is paid to persuade the public to develop sales-resistance to things they don't need. Stores, to me, are places which display most of the things I can do without.

Second, we decided to give at least ten percent of our income to the congregation where we are members. While we have never earned the average family income in any community in which we have lived, we have gradually through the years increased our giving to a percentage considerably beyond the tithe. One blessing of giving is that today we truly find it easier to give than to spend on ourselves. Another blessing from God is that, in over forty years of marriage, we have never needed to pay a bill late.

Third, we agreed never to buy anything that begins to lose value immediately when it is purchased, unless we have the cash to pay for it. This has meant that we did not own a car until our second year of marriage when we were both twenty-five. At that point—long ago!—we bought a car for two hundred fifty dollars which lasted through graduate school. For us this decision meant that we did not buy anything without cash except our house and our education. This may seem like an impossible standard. But it worked for us and wasn't a hardship.

Fourth, as I explained in an earlier section, we agreed early in our marriage that before we bought anything costing more than fifty dollars, we would first discuss it. That practice has certainly been increasingly important in our learning to work together in the whole area of money. It has helped us build trust, togetherness, and security.

Fifth, although we have several credit cards which we carry primarily for unexpected needs and for travel, we have agreed that if we find ourselves paying interest on those balances, we will cut up the cards.

While each couple must be firmly persuaded in their own minds about what they want to do, we can testify that for us these choices have been enriching in every way. They have released us of the financial burdens which so many married people carry, producing stress in all their relationships.

### *For further thought:*

*What kind of agreement are you ready to make with your spouse about the getting, giving, saving, and spending of your money?*

# X.

# Keep the Triangle Strong

# 1.
# *The Triangle of Marriage*

"Unless the Lord builds the house, those who build it labor in vain" (Psalm 127:1). "A threefold cord is not quickly broken" (Ecclesiastes 4:12).

Research teams have studied many marriages in order to identify what factors make for permanence in marriage. Many agree that one of the most important elements is for a couple to have happily married parents. None of us can do much about that. We can, however, *determine* to be happily married, and there *is* much we can do about that, regardless of what background we come from.

A second major factor in holding a marriage together is a couple's active church participation. Only a small percentage of marriages which had active church affiliation were terminated. One of the strongest reasons for permanence in these religious marriages is the couple's expectation that marriage is for life.

Imagine marriage as a triangle with God at the top. The closer a husband and wife move toward God, the closer they are drawn to each other.

In addition, if life teaches us anything, it is that we need a purpose beyond ourselves. In no relationship is this realization more necessary than in marriage.

Praying together is vital. And the promise of Christ is that, "If two of you shall agree in prayer as touching anything, it shall be done of my Father which is in heaven." That is a call to prayer for every Christian married couple.

The *Chicago Catholic* reported on a national survey in which approximately half of all marriages end in divorce. However, among couples who attend church regularly, only one in fifty marriages terminates in divorce. Furthermore, among couples who practice an active prayer life together, the rate is one divorce in 1,105 marriages.

Leland Foster Wood writes, "The pair who pray will lay hold on sources of power and understanding greater than their own, and will gain for their home something of the strength and serenity of God himself."

A couple who is committed to faith will find that reading the Bible together will sustain their spiritual life in much the same way as food sustains their physical life. It is impossible to grow spiritually without a growing understanding and response to the Scripture. It holds the guidance we need.

A couple who is serious about being faithful Christians will discover the value in attending church regularly and participating actively in the program of the church. For spiritual development, we all need the fellowship of God's people. We can't expect to receive the encouragement and enrichment we need without attending and fellowshiping with others who love and serve God. Statistics are clear that those who are active in the church will, almost without exception, have the resources to remain married.

A marriage benefits when a couple worships together. The very act of sitting side by side in worship joins partners in a wonderful oneness. It is quite possible for a husband and wife to participate actively in different congregations, just as it is possible for one of them to eat in the dining room and the other to eat in the kitchen. But it is not the ideal way to live.

It is essential that a husband and wife are together in the great spiritual realities. This is one of the reasons why I have insisted over the years that both join one church and commit themselves to one congregation *before* the wedding. Afterward it becomes a real struggle.

Again and again I have found that Christian young people as they approach marriage intend to pray together, go to church together, read the Bible together, and generally share spiritual activities. Yet often, even in the most diligent families, these practices don't happen, at least with any regularity.

So what is needed? A commitment to pray together, to read the Bible together, and to faithfully worship and work together in the church. Without that commitment, the spiritual soon takes second, third, or fourth place, or is dropped completely.

On the other hand, when couples make a commitment along these lines and promise together to give them priority in their marriages, they usually do follow through, and their marriages and families are blessed.

In a wonderfully warm way, the well-known French doctor and counselor Paul Tournier writes in the book, *Marriages That Work,* about how he and his wife Nelly learned spiritual oneness. In the chapter, "The Spiritual Foundation of Marital Success," Dr. Tournier says, "So we have continued, at least once a week for more than forty years, these three-way meetings: God, Nelly and I. This conjugal meditation compliments personal meditation and vice versa. My whole career and my life's work followed as a result of it." Tournier says, "There needs to be a drawing near to God by the husband and wife who together have resolved to keep listening to Him."

Joshua of old made an exemplary commitment when he said, "As for me and my house, we will serve the Lord."

**For further thought:**

> Before you were married, what did you assume that you and your spouse would do together spiritually? Which of those assumptions have you actually done? Which have you not done?

# 2.

# *A Sacred Covenant*

George Macdonald, the Scottish writer of a century ago, said to his wife, "My dearest, when I love God more, I love you the way you ought to be loved." I know that is true.

I have put the matter of our relation to God toward the end of the book, not because it is the least important of the subjects, but because it is the basis of all the others.

At the wedding of Princess Elizabeth and Phillip, Geoffrey Fisher, Archbishop of Canterbury, told the royal couple, "The ever-living Christ is here to bless you. The nearer you keep to Him the nearer you will be to the other."

Betty and I have found this to be true. We entered marriage believing that God had led us together and that our commitment was first to God and then to each other. And we've experienced happiness and meaning in our marriage in proportion to our practice of that commitment.

Our wish to serve God faithfully and our common Christian commitment have helped us to choose the places we have served, to use our money, and to conduct our interpersonal relationships with integrity. We fell short many times, and our priorities were not always as clear as they ought to have been, but our basic commitment helped us work through failures and find forgiveness and faith again.

We also know many marriages which have experienced

new life or have moved from the mediocre to the meaningful by renewing their commitment to seek God's direction and then follow that.

A good marriage is not so much a contract between two persons as a sacred covenant between three—God, wife, and husband. Without this kind of primary relationship with God, the strength and stability of any marriage is considerably weakened.

Hazen G. Werner wrote, "Family love and understanding are made complete when God is there. The lives of all members of the family depend on the ultimate good: life with God."

If we were beginning our marriage again, we would continually remind ourselves to keep the triangle strong. We would covenant with each other from the start to practice attitudes and actions which place God at the center of our home.

Like most Christian couples, we assumed that after we were married we would naturally pray and read the Bible together every day. Like many other couples, however, we soon realized that our being Christians didn't make these practices happen automatically. And although we prayed regularly before each meal and now and then at other times, we were praying together less than we meant to.

We skipped sometimes because our schedule changed or we didn't plan adequately or we ran out of time. Yet we knew we were missing the greatest blessings promised to even two people who will ask anything in the name of Jesus. The precious promise of God's answer when two people pray is not only for persons at a church prayer meeting, but also for a husband and wife who pray together.

We have learned that not only is it possible to claim and receive God's promise as a married couple, but it is a responsibility and a privilege given us by our Lord. Praying as a couple is one of the great gifts of marriage. Yet it is a gift married people seldom claim.

**For further thought:**
> *What place has prayer and reading the Scripture together had in your marriage? What place would each of you like them to have?*

# 3.
# The Danger of Neglect

Why do we not pick up the privileges of prayer and reading God's word? Simple neglect is probably the biggest reason. We just don't plan for them to be as much a part of our lives as eating and working. Furthermore, these practices require honesty. We can't have problems in our relationships and pray with meaning and reality. That may be one reason why the Bible warns us not to have a spirit of bitterness against our spouse. Such a spirit hinders prayer.

After I finished leading a session on marriage, a couple came forward to talk. They were smiling as they explained that they had attended a marriage seminar I had led earlier in another state. "When you read the Scripture which says, 'Never go to bed mad because if you do, you give the devil a chance to do his work,' we went home and promised together to live that way. It's revolutionized our marriage. It's also been a spiritual renewal for us."

Never go to bed angry or bitter, says the Scripture. Nowhere is this instruction more needed than in our marriages and families. To let wrong feelings and attitudes drag into bedtime means that only harm can come. Small differences and difficulties have the capacity to smolder into tremendous anger and distrust which tear true lovers apart. Love can survive large problems which are faced and dealt with openly better than small ones which simmer, hidden inside.

Why else do we fail to exercise the privileges of praying

and reading Scripture together? The values of power, money, and self-gratification which surround us easily crowd out our intention to live God-centered lives. A selfish spirit and the spirit of Christ are contrary to each other.

We know that to make marriage work we need God to be a key player. A marriage needs forgiveness and God makes forgiveness possible. A marriage needs grace, which means that we receive more good things than we deserve, and God makes us gracious, giving persons. A marriage needs mercy, which means that judgment is withheld when we deserve to be punished. And God gives us mercy for ourselves and for each other.

I believe also that a marriage needs the broader fellowship of God's people. If we are to have a firm faith, we need support from and interchange with God's family, the church.

God knows we need a body of persons to help and encourage us in the right way, surrounded as we are by those elements which threaten marriages.

### For further thought:

> *How essential do you believe it is never to go to bed with a bitter spirit or without clearing up any misunderstanding? How possible do you believe that is?*

# 4.
# Scriptures about Divorce

Whenever Jesus responded to a question about marriage and divorce, he returned to God's original ideal for creation: that one man and one woman are joined together for life.

As individual Christians, and as the church, we are called to live and support this ideal. No other institution in society will remind people of God's gift if the church fails to hold it before everyone who enters marriage.

Let us continue to declare that the only sexual union which benefits humankind, and which the Scripture recognizes, is the joining of one man and one woman for life. The only reason for divorce that the Scripture grants is when there has been infidelity. And even then divorce is not preferred. Rather, repentance and reconciliation is the way God intends. There is not much humility or tenderness or forgiveness present when a divorce is underway.

Here are Scriptures from the New Testament which every person who is planning to marry, as well as every married person, should consider seriously from time to time.

"To the married I give this command—not I, but the Lord—that the wife should not separate from her husband (but if she does separate, let her remain unmarried or else be reconciled to her husband), and that the husband should not divorce his wife" (I Corinthians 7:10, 11).

In Matthew's Gospel Jesus says, "It was also said, 'Whoever divorces his wife, let him give her a certificate of divorce,' but I say to you that anyone who divorces his wife, except on the grounds of unchastity, causes her to commit adultery and whoever marries a divorced woman commits adultery" (Matthew 5:31, 32).

Since Matthew's Gospel is the only one with the exception clause "except for unchastity," biblical scholars are inclined to feel that this was inserted to match contemporary Jewish thought. The other Gospels and Romans do not have this exception.

"He said to them, 'Whoever divorces his wife and marries another commits adultery against her; and if she divorces her husband and marries another, she commits adultery'" (Mark 10:11, 12). "'Anyone who divorces his wife and marries another commits adultery, and whoever marries a woman divorced from her husband commits adultery'" (Luke 16:18).

"Some Pharisees came to him and to test him they asked, 'Is it lawful for a man to divorce his wife for any cause?' He answered, 'Have you not read that the one who made them at the beginning "made them male and female," and said, "For this reason a man shall leave his father and mother and be joined to his wife, and the two shall become one flesh"? So they are no longer two, but one flesh. Therefore, what God has joined together, let no one separate.' They said to him, 'Why then did Moses command us to give a certificate of dismissal and to divorce her?' He said to them, 'It was because you were so hardhearted that Moses allowed you to divorce your wives, but from the beginning it was not so. And I say to you, whoever divorces his wife, except for unchastity, and marries another commits adultery'" (Matthew 19:3-9).

"Do you not know, brothers and sisters—for I am speaking to those who know the law—that the law is binding on a person only during that person's lifetime? Thus, a married woman is bound by the law to her husband as long as he lives; but if her husband dies, she is discharged from the law concerning the husband. Accordingly, she will be called an adulteress if she lives with another man while her husband is alive, But if her husband dies, she is free from that law, and, if she marries another man, she is not an adulteress" (Romans 7:1-3).

Even when the Scriptures acknowledge divorce, they do not sanction remarriage after divorce. If this were fully understood and believed, I am sure there would be considerably fewer quick divorces.

God's ideal is always one man and one woman joined together for life. If one spouse becomes a Christian, the Scripture urges the Christian not to initiate a separation.

"To the rest I say—I and not the Lord—that if any believer has a wife who is an unbeliever, and she consents to live with him, he should not divorce her. And if any woman has a husband who is an unbeliever, and he consents to live with her, she should not divorce him. For the unbelieving husband is made holy through his wife, and the unbelieving wife is made holy through her husband. Otherwise your children would be unclean, but, as it is, they are holy. But if the unbelieving partner separates, let it be so; in such a case the brother or sister is not bound. It is to peace that God has called you. Wife, for all you know, you might save your husband. Husband, for all you know, you might save your wife" (I Corinthians 7:12-16).

I realize that these passages describe God's ideal. They do not deal with failure in marriage. But this is what the Scriptures say. We must talk about failure in another kind of discussion.

Even though in North America divorce is granted for nearly every conceivable reason, and many counselors are quick to suggest separation and divorce, as Christians we are responsible to hold up God's ideal, even while we continue to be redemptive when there is failure.

**For further thought:**
> What do these Scriptures say to you about marriage? About divorce? About remarriage?

# 5.
# *The Trouble with Divorce*

The old wedding vows stated, "For better or for worse, till death do us part." But in the last several decades there have been revisions. Some promise "through good times or bad," or, as a young man said in a seminar, "We'll never do it like our parents did. We only promise to live together as long as we love." My comment was, "I'll give you six months on that one. Sometimes it doesn't take even six months until you may wonder if you love or not." When those times come, it will be the commitment for life that pulls you through to the fulfilling years ahead, realized only by those who have the fortitude and determination to stay together.

Of those divorced persons who remarry, sixty-five percent will divorce again. And if children are involved in the marriage, seventy-five percent will divorce the second time. Statistics don't measure the loneliness, guilt, despair, and brokenness that are part of the whole divorce experience. But those emotions can nearly overtake those who go through this death-like event.

A consensus of studies reported in *The New York Times* says that divorced persons have substantially higher rates of emotional problems, accidental death, suicide, and death from heart disease, cancer, pneumonia, high blood pressure, and cirrhosis of the liver. Divorce causes more damage to emotional and physical health than virtually any other stress, including widowhood. Divorce is a kind of living death. Researchers tell us that not enough attention has been given to how divorce affects former spouses.

A powerful book which every person considering divorce should read carefully is *The Case Against Divorce,* written by Diane Medved, a marriage counselor and psychologist.

Medved, who formerly thought of divorce as morally neutral, now speaks of divorce as irreparably damaging to the very people she wanted to help.

"Often in tears, the divorced people I talked with described fantasies of a spouse returning or confessed guilt over abandoning a devoted mate. They spoke of being uprooted from their house, of splitting possessions, of children changed from innocents to confidants or scapegoats. And they mourned a part of their lives never to be recaptured—the family unit destroyed."

When asked the question, "Could you have made it work?" both sides usually confess, "Yes, we could have made it work."

We live in an atmosphere of disposable marriages and with fantasies kept alive by entertainment that divorce will open up new horizons, that other brighter, happier, more lovable people are out there. But each time we take ourselves with us. And multitudes of the married-again see too late that what they had in their first relationship was best. What they lost in spouse, children, and extended family is irretrievable.

Author Medved now stresses that marriage is for keeps, not just until passion fades. In a time when persons expect instant satisfaction, she pleads for couples to "work to build a future" rather than to live only in the here and now. Medved stresses that "divorce is shameful failure" and needs to be recognized as such.

Finally, author Medved points out that the last several decades introduced a wave of self-centeredness which had a woeful effect on marriage and family. What was formerly considered illicit behavior is now justified under an explanation of openness and honesty. And the results are evident all around.

One women's magazine survey of 350,000 readers revealed that 83.4 percent of wives who were unfaithful eventually divorced. Philip Blumstein and Pepper Schwartz in *American Couples* note, "Husbands and wives who have had extramarital sex were more likely to break up, whether it happened at the beginning of their marriage or after many years. In marriage, non-monogamy is such a trespass that even those in established relationships do not shut their eyes."

If there is to be love in marriage, and if there are to be strong families, then we Christians, of all persons, must revive and practice those virtues that foster faithful, stable, happy homes.

### For further thought:
*What myths do you think people are susceptible to when they ponder divorce?*

# 6.
## Imagine What Happens

I have learned to ask a couple who is considering divorce to imagine what's ahead. The couple should visualize in vivid detail what their lives will be like after they divorce.

Separation and divorce are never only the concern of two people. The pain, stigma, and ramifications reach far and are lifelong.

Imagine first what happens to you and your spouse. Breaking a fundamental relationship leaves scars for life, and sometimes the open wounds never heal. One is never the same.

Imagine how happy you will be after all is said and done. In a ten-year study of sixty divorced couples conducted by Judith Wallerstein, Executive Director of the Center for Family in Transition in Corte Madera, California, the findings were simple but sad: only ten percent of couples felt that both the husbands' and wives' lives had improved.

Consider carefully the loneliness of life after divorce. Many times the loneliness is worse than death because the partners live on but are dead to each other. Loneliness is one of the key marks of our time. Even when marriages and families are separated in spirit, utter loneliness can take over, causing persons to act in strange, even devious, ways, in their effort to find companionship and someone to care.

Imagine the loss and the destroyed dreams which divorce always brings. Not only are promises and vows broken, but so are the hopes and dreams of a lifetime commitment.

Then review some of your happiest times, your most loving times together. Remembering happiness always points one's mind toward the prospect of similar happiness in the future. If a husband and wife can form a clear, steady image of the kind of marriage which is possible, many times—with help—they can work through difficulties and see hope again.

Imagine the effect of a divorce upon your children. It is not true, as some counselors tell parents, that the children will adjust easily. Some may appear to do so, but nearly all live with deep scars. The children in the conflict carry feelings of guilt, thinking they are, at least in part, the cause for the separation. Many children live the rest of their lives with a sense that something essential is missing, that they were somehow deserted and robbed of love. They feel the long-term effects particularly keenly on special occasions such as high school graduations, weddings, and family reunions.

While one might argue that children are damaged by living in the presence of an unhappy or unhealthy marriage, one must also recognize that divorce is seldom, if ever, kinder. Any couple contemplating divorce should concretely imagine the effects now and in the future upon the children and grandchildren caught in the middle of such an action.

Imagine what happens in each of your families on both sides of the divorce. The family of each spouse is deeply involved in the happiness, unhappiness, emotional, and even physical, results of such a separation. Family and friends are all affected, now and in the years to come, by the waves of remorse which reach everyone related to those who divorce.

Imagine also what happens, even if we refuse to believe it, in the world around us—in our work, our religious life, and our relationships with persons in our community. While divorce is easy from a legal standpoint, its emotional impact is deeply disturbing—to a wide range of related persons. And the side-effects—depression, feelings of failure, and low self-esteem—can last a lifetime.

The partners in many happy marriages considered separation or divorce at some time. But happiness doesn't come by dodging problems. We mature, and love matures, as we face our problems and grow in overcoming them.

**For further thought:**

*Are there other areas of life, or other persons, which a couple who is considering divorce should imagine?*

# 7.
## For Stability and Strength

While we know that going to church, praying, and reading the Bible do not guarantee a successful marital relationship, we know also that each of these brings considerable stability to a marriage. Whenever we strengthen these practices, our lives are enlarged and all our relationships are enriched. Betty and I have learned from experience that faithfulness in these areas bears the fruit of love, joy, and peace.

We are more sure today than ever that God led us together because we continue to see God's leading in a thousand ways. When we seek God's guidance together and then follow God's way, we are doubly assured that we are in God's will. We have the witness of each other.

We know the privilege of praying together about plans and needs in our own lives and on behalf of others. We know the joy of sharing God's power together. We do not feel alone in our spiritual walk because we know we have the support of each other, whether we are together or whether we are physically separated. All this is God's gift to any of us who keep the triangle strong.

We have learned in our walk with God that to live and love does not involve only looking into each other's eyes. It means also looking out together, serving beyond ourselves, lifting the loads of others, and helping to meet the needs of those next to us and beyond. Some of our most meaningful and happy moments in our marriage have been when we joined hands in prayer and worked for the blessing of others.

No two persons can live only for each other. Life's meaning becomes clearer when we look out in the same direction to serve in a cause greater than ourselves.

In his article "Christian Marriage: A New Vocation" Orin N. Hutchinson, Jr. says, "Marriage becomes more than just a couple's coming together to meet each other's needs and to seek mutual enjoyment. From the Christian perspective, marriage can become a means to an end. The end is bigger than the marriage: What difference can the two of you make in the life of the world? Whom can you help? What caring can you bring? What causes serve?"

With this kind of an example, our children become useful persons in our world. Only as they witness selfless living can they absorb a spirit of selflessness. In this way our homes become spiritual launching platforms from which we send our children out to serve the world.

Yes, we've discovered that when we are close to God, we are close to each other. When we are close to each other, we find it easy to make contact with God and others.

### For further thought:

*What dangers do we face if we focus only on meeting each other's needs and do not look out together to serve others?*

# 8.
# A God-Centered Home

Years ago in Greenland, legend has it, when a stranger knocked at the door, the visitor asked, "Is God in this house?"

Some Christians in years past set an extra place at the dinner table for Christ. In this way they invited Christ to be present and also reminded themselves that Christ was a member of their family.

Shortly after Dr. G. Campbell Morgan was married, his parents visited the newlyweds' home and were given a tour of the house. At the conclusion his father expressed appreciation for the visit and tour, but he said that he didn't see anything in the house which told him it was a Christian home. Dr. Morgan was so struck with this that later he wrote about it, stating that it was true. There was nothing to indicate to visitors that he and his wife were Christians. From then on they decided that their house should speak of their faith, that the very walls and rooms would somehow communicate their commitment to Christ.

I have just returned from visiting a friend, and I will not soon forget the impression the house gave me. When I arrived, I noticed small candles in the windows. My friend explained that these are friendship candles and that they have them turned on day and night. Then I learned too that since this family moved into the area, their home has become known throughout the city and surrounding countryside because of the candles. In fact, they have had many contacts with persons simply because of the small candles in the windows.

Christian sentiment is fine, but it isn't enough. May everything about our lives and homes speak of our faith in God.

No material inheritance can compare in value to the influence and blessing of a home where love and faith are practiced. Those qualities have consequence for time and eternity; they are seldom denied or disowned.

**For further thought:**

> *What about your home tells people that it is a Christian home?*

# 9.
# Heirs Together
# of the Grace of Life

"You are heirs together of the grace of life" (I Peter 3:7).

I find this phrase—"heirs together of the grace of life"—to be one of the most beautiful in all the literature of the church. It forms a perfect conclusion to a discussion about what Christian marriage is and can be.

Grace means that we receive blessings beyond what we deserve. For husbands and wives it can include all the benefits and blessings we receive as we live in love and consideration of each other. In fact, we will receive much more than we expect or are worthy of, just as the word "grace" implies.

The phrase includes our experience of togetherness. We are heirs together. We experience God's grace not only alone, but also together. God's blessings are increased when we share them together. Our fears are halved and our blessings are multiplied as we live for God.

The statement means that in marriage, our religious life is not the responsibility of only one of the partners who sees that religious duties are performed, that prayer is said, that children go to church and are taught the Scripture. Marriage means that we work *together* in spiritual matters, and that we experience the fullness of God's grace when we are together in this area of life.

We are heirs. Heirs keep coming into their inheritances

as time moves on. In that way, there are always greater riches and greater gifts as we each take God into our marriage. At that rate, on our fiftieth anniversary we'll be even fuller and richer then we can now imagine.

To live together as heirs of God's grace means that, in a real sense, we are keepers of each other's souls. The closeness of marriage can drive persons farther from God if the two partners are not first of all committed to God. When that commitment is clear, it affects all our other commitments.

Augustine saw the final purpose of marriage as being "that the one may bring the other with him to heaven." Whether we get closer or farther from God depends upon how we help or hinder each other in our routine lives. And one of our greatest responsibilities as Christians is to faithfully practice our commitment to God in our marriages. Our marriage relationship and our salvation are interwoven in the way in which we respond to each other and to the grace of God.

In a fine book, *So You Are Going to Be Married*, Dr. Clair Amstutz, a family physician for many years, wrote, "Finally, the conviction has been slowly growing that the spiritual aspects of marriage are more important than the biological ones. This idea came slowly because all American literature on marriage stressed the physical with emphasis on anatomy and physiology, and that was my particular training . . . I thought I was making an original discovery when I saw that those who have great spiritual resources generally have no problem of 'incompatibility.'"

In marriage, the more we seek to please God, the more we want to please each other. The more honest and open we are with God, the more honest and open we are able to be with each other. On the other hand, if we do not demonstrate honesty, oneness, and love for each other, we cannot long remain honest, open, and in love with God.

God is the great savior, God is the great healer, God is the great helper. We who acknowledge God will know that continual saving power. We will experience that healing of many hurts. We will know the inexpressible joy of kneeling together in prayer and going on together, strengthened for whatever life brings, to be servants together.

It is a blessed privilege to live together as heirs of the grace of life!

### *For further thought:*

> *What specific blessings do you believe Christian wives and husband can receive as "heirs together"?*

# XI.

# It Is Never Too Late

# 1.
# *Beginning Again*

No marriage is completely unique. In fact, problems in marriages are often very similar. Whether we succeed or fail in our marriages usually depends more on how we deal with our problems, than on the fact that we have them.

In our forty-plus years of marriage we have needed to begin again and again. There were times when our communication seemed to be meaningless and at a standstill. We talked about those things that we needed to talk about in order to live in the same house. At times we each felt lonely and unloved. Now and then we wondered about our love and whether we might be happier had we married someone else. During the difficult years of child-rearing and the disappointments of children straying, we were tempted to deal with the strain by blaming each other.

In spite of all of these experiences—or because of them—we know that even the most difficult experiences of life can be doors to new beginnings, new understandings, and growth in greater love than we ever imagined at the start of our marriage.

In many areas of our life together we are past the place of beginning again. For example, our children are grown and gone, so it is impossible for us to start over with rearing and nurturing them. We have given as much as we can to their growing up years; now our major contribution is to stand by and be available when they need us. The fact that we can't correct our past mistakes or re-do our child-rearing makes every parent sad to one degree or another. Who of us hasn't said, "If I had it to do over, I would do it differently"?

But marriage is different. As long as we have breath, we have the possibility of beginning again. We can still put all these ideas and ideals into practice. Any marriage can be changed and improved if the partners will to change and improve. We need not be resigned to a static or unsatisfactory relationship.

William J. Lederere and Don D. Jackson in *Mirages of Marriage* wrote, "Somehow, a myth has arisen in this country which teaches that the first few years of marriage form the period during which all problems get ironed out. The implication seems to be that thereafter the spouses sit passively while the marital wagon rolls along through life. This conception of the relationship is nonsense . . . Divorce figures indicate how fallacious this myth really is. Interviews with hundreds of couples clearly show that those who resign themselves to a static relationship are inviting divorce, desertion, or disaster. Disaster comes in many forms in marriage, from psychosomatic and mental illness all the way to the grim life of the Gruesome Twosome."

### For further thought:

*What would you do differently if you were beginning your marriage again? Regardless of your current stage, do you believe it is possible to begin again right where you are?*

# 2.
# *Change Is Always Possible*

Perhaps you recall the woman who told a marriage counselor that she not only wants out of her marriage, she wants to make her husband suffer as much as possible.

"You really want to hurt him?" the counselor asked.

"Yes, I do. He's hurt me so much I want revenge."

"I'd suggest this strategy if you want to hurt him. Divorcing him may not hurt him at all. He may be glad to get rid of you. For the next month, butter him up. Do special little things for him. Make him meals he especially enjoys. Act kindly and say kind things. Then just as he begins to respond, hit him with the divorce. I guarantee he'll be deeply hurt."

A month or more went by. By chance the counselor saw the woman again. "Did you take my advice?" the counselor asked. "Yes, I did," she replied. "And did you sue for divorce?" "No," answered the woman. "We are deeply in love."

The happy marriage is made by those who believe that change is always possible and that life is always improvable. In a happy marriage, partners have the will to change and to adjust to each other's needs and feelings. In a happy marriage, spouses learn to give and take so that their relationship grows in vitality and meaning.

André Maurois described it this way: "A successful marriage is an edifice that must be rebuilt every day." One can look at such building of a marriage as drudgery and utter toil. Those who see marriage in this light haven't yet experienced the joy of working together or discovered the beautiful dwelling God intends marriage to be.

I believe marriage is an edifice which we build every day. Each of us decides the beauty of the building we live in. We are building for each other the kind of house we will live in. Sometimes we realize that part of the structure is weak and needs strengthening. At other times we need to do some remodeling to make the house more useful or safe or serviceable. Now and then we notice that we should make repairs if the house is not to crumble. All these actions are necessary in marriage.

But like a builder, we don't only do repairs. We know the joy of designing something beautiful which is a pleasure to live in—where to place the windows for the best view, for example. All this is the possibility of marriage.

**For further thought:**
> *How open are you to change?*

# 3.

# *To Love Is to Forgive*

The kindest and the happiest pair
Will find occasion to forbear;
And something, every day they live,
To pity, and perhaps forgive.

William Cowper

Robert Louis Stevenson wrote, "To marry is to domesticate the recording angel." The simple words "I remember what you did" or "I remember what you said" are barbs which hurt. Remembering your partner's mistakes is a practice which can wreck your marriage. Marriage is impossible and unbearable if you aren't willing to forgive and forget. You have no hope for happiness if you harbor hurt feelings or thoughts. Yet it is on this very point that many marriages shipwreck.

"The truth is that the whole fellowship of marriage is ultimately based on forgiveness," says David R. Mace in *Whom God Has Joined.* "Two people unable to forgive cannot endure to live together as a married couple. That is why the courts are so clumsy and so helpless in dealing with marriage problems. The law is concerned with offense and retribution, with neatly balanced justice that makes the punishment fit the crime. In grave matters this principle may be necessary to keep the peace, but so long as marriage remains in any sense a relationship, it must be conducted upon an entirely different principle—the principle of repentance and forgiveness."

This forgiveness is not some cheap pronouncement which wants to wash away every conflict, that glibly dismisses the incident as if it were nothing. That is not true forgiveness. Rather, it is as I Corinthians 13:5 describes it: "Love does not keep an account of evil" (J.B. Phillips translation).

Or one might paraphrase it: "Love does not keep a list of mistakes." Love wipes the slate clean.

Refusing to forgive can be a kind of control, manipulating the other, trying to compel the other to knuckle under. It is a force against marriage and true love.

A happy marriage is not a *perfect* marriage, because no one is perfect. Everyone makes mistakes, breaks things, hurts others, and gets in one kind of difficulty or another. But a happy marriage is made up of mature persons who freely forgive and forget. Without this forgiveness, they will have distress, unhappiness, and regret.

Settling a difficult situation as soon as possible has emotional, physical, and spiritual benefits. The strain of inner hostility or unforgiveness is too great for any of us to bear without serious repercussions. It can show up in the rest of our relationships; it is reflected in our whole emotional and physical well-being.

In an address on marriage, one speaker commented that he doubts that any couple who holds inner resentments will celebrate their fiftieth wedding anniversary. The strain of such living is too severe, and it takes its toll not only in stifling relationships, but in shortening life.

None of us can have a happy marriage if we let little irritations linger within, if we hold grudges, or if we allow anger and resentment to destroy the fiber of our lives. Although it is difficult to discuss our deep, real problems and feelings, it is the best medicine for healing a marriage and making it strong. The question is not, will we ever be angry and bitter with each other. The question is whether we will deal with those feelings and their causes as soon as possible.

Sometimes the spirit of unforgiveness which destroys a marriage has its roots outside the marriage itself. Persons who are unwilling to forgive their parents or others can find that their past plays havoc in the present. Donald Hope, a psychotherapist, recalls working with a young husband and father for eight months. They got nowhere. Tom hated his alcoholic father intensely. No counseling could soften his sickening memories. No words could relieve his rage. And, meanwhile, his spirit of bitterness spilled out over his wife, his children, and co-workers.

One night Tom's pastor suggested that he forgive his father. They knelt and prayed. Tom made a remarkable recovery. The next day he told his father, "Last night I asked God to help me forgive you, and I think maybe it worked."

Tom's father embraced him and began to cry. A transforming experience happened. Not only did Tom's spirit change, but he became a gentle, kind, and loving husband and father. What a vast amount of professional counseling could not do, forgiveness did.

The greatest sin may be not what has been done against us. The most devastating sin may be our unwillingness to forgive the person who has wronged us.

Forgiveness is not first a feeling. It is fundamentally a promise. When we forgive, we promise to:

- Never bring it up again or use it against the other.
- Look for ways to do good to the one we forgive.
- Refuse to talk with others about the situation.
- Refuse to continually dwell on the wrong that's been done.

One way to begin to feel right toward another is to begin

to do right toward that person. In the same way, it may be necessary to say "I forgive you," and mean it as much as is possible, in order to begin restoring trust and love. Not to forgive will kill the best marriage and the deepest love.

### For further thought:

> *A marriage cannot exist without forgiveness. Are you able to forgive and forget? If not—why not?*

# 4.
# *Like Building a Beautiful House*

Certainly repairs will be needed in every marriage. And change will always come. But there is the ongoing excitement of building something beautiful which can be joyfully shared with others. A marriage is blessed when, like a beautiful house, it is a joy to dwell in together and when other persons can come and go from it peacefully.

We have found this to be true. We have learned that the romance of courtship is nothing compared to the romance of love which grows through the years in deep understanding and acceptance. We know that the dwelling we live in is one we have built together. There are flaws in it because we lacked the artisan's knowledge, and there are marks in the material because we didn't always use the tools correctly. And yet we have been happy because we designed corners for closeness and placed windows so that we could look out together on the world. We have created this together, and so we have the satisfaction of feeling like owners.

If we were beginning our marriage, we would make a commitment to change, to grow, to do those things God shows us which make a greater marriage. We would realize from the start that as long as God gives us breath, we have the opportunity to begin again.

For my final words I share a poem I wrote to my wife, Betty. In it are a commitment, a compliment, and a prayer.

## To My Love

My love,
I love you with a steadfast love
That's true and deep,
Which flows forth from full faith
In your love and worth—
Beyond the sentiment and insight
Of early love.

I love you
For the stability and strength
Your understanding gives
In times of failure and reverses;
For the hope which you hold out
When mistakes are made;
And when others give up.

My love,
May God grant me,
Unspoken or expressed,
Such love for you
That thanksgiving will not cease
To Him for you,
His gift to me.

**For further thought:**

*Think of marriage as the builder of an edifice that is much more beautiful and has greater possibilities than any physical house or property.*

*What kind of dwelling are you building? Describe its beauty or the beauty which you would like it to have.*

*Where does it need repair?*

# *About the Author*

**John M. Drescher**, Quakertown, PA has been a writer, editor, pastor, and seminary teacher. He is married to Betty Keener. They have five married children and thirteen grandchildren.

Drescher has authored thirty-seven books, of which more than a dozen relate to husband and wife, and parent and child relationships. **Seven Things Children Need** is now printed in twenty languages. **If I Were Starting My Family Again** was condensed in *Readers Digest*. Other books include **When Your Child Is 6 to 12, Meditations For the Newly Married, Doing What Comes Spiritually, If I Were Starting My Ministry Again, Now Is The Time To Love, Invocations and Benedictions for the Revised Common Lectionary,** and **Parents—Passing the Torch of Faith.**

Drescher has written for more than 100 different magazines. He has spoken widely to conventions, retreats, and seminars, often on the subjects of family and spiritual renewal.

**Group Discounts**

# *For the Love of Marriage*
# ORDER FORM

If you would like to order multiple copies of *For the Love of Marriage* for groups you are a part of, use this form. (Discounts apply only for more than one copy.)

Photocopy this page as often as you like.

---

### *The following discounts apply:*

| | |
|---:|:---|
| 1 copy | $9.95 |
| 2-5 copies | $8.95 each (a 10% discount) |
| 6-10 copies | $8.45 each (a 15% discount) |
| 11-20 copies | $7.96 each (a 20% discount) |

*Prices subject to change.*

---

*Quantity*                                                    Price        Total

____ copies of **For the Love of Marriage**  @ _____ _____

PA residents add 6% sales tax _____

Shipping & Handling
*(add 10%, $3.00 minimum)* _____

TOTAL _____

*(Please fill in the payment and
shipping information on the other side.)*

**Group Discounts for _For the Love of Marriage_**

# METHOD OF PAYMENT

❑ Check or Money Order
(payable to Good Books in U.S. funds)

❑ Please charge my:
  ❑ MasterCard  ❑ Visa  ❑ Discover

\# _____

exp. date _____

Signature _____

Name _____

Address _____

City _____

State _____

Zip _____

Phone Number _____

SHIP TO: (if different)

Name _____

Address _____

City _____

State _____

Zip _____

**Mail order to**
  **Good Books,** P.O. Box 419, Intercourse, PA 17534-0419
  Call toll-free 800/762-7171
  Fax toll-free 888/768-3433

_Prices subject to change._